THE SOLAR COOKERY BOOK

THE SOLAR COOKERY BOOK

Everything Under The Sun

Beth and Dan Halacy

Peace Press
1978

© 1978 Peace Press Inc.

Peace Press
3828 Willat Avenue
Culver City, California 90230

Printed in the United States of America
by Peace Press

Library of Congress Catalog Number: 77-17686
International Standard Book Number: 0-915238-21-7

9 8 7 6 5 4 3 2 1

We dedicate this book to
Deirdre, Jessica, Paul, Boom, and Zack.

ACKNOWLEDGEMENTS

Dan thanks his good friend Herb Wade for the many drawings in the book. Beth is particularly indebted to her dear friend, Coralee Woody, who not only shared several of her wonderful recipes, but also took a solar oven home and tested recipes. Other fine cooks who have given Beth recipes or help for this book include Peggy Akin, Jay Blackshaw, Joe Costion, Jessica Fernandez, Helen Good, Jean Goodwin, Helios, Edith Hill, Dee Latimer, Loretta Larson, Jessica Koory, Betty Miller, Bonnie Peploe, Bess Rice, Mary Saylor, Bob and Janet Steelman, and Laura Woods.

TABLE OF CONTENTS

Twenty years ago we used the Umbroiler, one of the first solar cookers available, to cook in an area where fire building was prohibited. We have developed our own cookers since then and use solar energy almost everyday to prepare our food.

PREFACE

We cooked our first solar meal more than twenty years ago, shortly after attending the First World Symposium on Solar Energy in Phoenix, Arizona. Since then we have continued to experiment with the sun's energy. An earlier book of Dan's described a number of easy-to-build solar projects, including solar cookers. *Solar Cookery* is entirely about solar cooking, and describes in detail how you can make your own solar oven and reflector hot plate, and how to cook with them.

Some commercial solar cookers are quite expensive, but the two we show you how to build in this book are not. Supplies for the solar oven can be bought for as little as twenty-five dollars. The cardboard and aluminum foil reflector cooker costs less than half that much. And if you are a good scrounger you may be able to build them for practically no cash outlay. Best of all, both projects can be built by amateurs. Neither of us qualify as experts with tools, but our solar cookers work very well. Some of the tougher parts of construction we simply "farmed out" to the local sheet metal shop.

The potential of solar cooking is unlimited. How about making solar coffee? Or sun-cooked bacon and eggs? Or steak? We can cook a turkey in the solar oven as fast as our electric oven can do it! The second part of *Solar Cookery* has recipes which have been tested on the solar cookers. You will be able to make entire meals, from soup to dessert, as easily and quickly as you can in the kitchen.

Solar cookery saves money too, but that isn't the main reason we enjoy it. Far more important is the fact that this kind of cooking is an excellent way to show the great potential of solar energy. The sun grows our food and can cook it as well; that same energy can heat water and keep our houses warm. Some day the sun may provide nearly all our energy — safe and unlimited energy that will clean up our environment and save precious gas and petroleum for better uses.

Solar Cookery is the first book available on how to harness the sun's energy in preparing food. Though this book will obviously appeal to the solar enthusiast it was not written with only that in mind. We believe that once people discover how easy, and how enjoyable solar cooking can be, the sun's energy will become a mainstay in food preparation. *Solar Cookery* will appeal to many kinds of people:

It is for people who are interested in conservation and a wise use of our resources, plus a desire to protect the environment.

It is for students who are searching for a new project for a science fair. It is also a basic information resource for students who want to learn more about the simple principles that make it possible to put the sun to work in so many useful ways.

It is for campers who want a way to cook safely in wooded areas without the need for a fire, or the nuisance of waiting for a fire to get going. No smoke, no ashes. Just clean, hot heat!

It is a new horizon for backyard barbecuers and cookout specialists.

It is for health advocates who are seeking ways to put their ideals to practical use. The higher nutritional value of solar cooked food will be a delight.

Perhaps most of all, it is for those who appreciate the fun and excitement of a new way of preparing food.

Maybe you are already a solar chef; we hope that is the case. Our cooking tips and recipes will be just as useful for other solar ovens and reflector cookers. We hope that you will like our book — and that almost all of your days will be sunny and your recipes turn out well!

Boy Scouts using a Fresnel lens to start a campfire. The solar cookers eliminate the need for a fire and are also educational.

INTRODUCTION

We have at last entered the age of solar energy, with solar water heaters, home heating and cooling in operation, and solar power plants soon to become a reality. Already there are hundreds of solar homes and buildings across the country. Perhaps there is one near you, or maybe you are one of the lucky people living in one! This harnessing of the sun's energy is happening largely because of the energy crisis. Solar energy is beginning to fill the gap left as fossil fuels dwindle. But there is another solar energy application that all of us can enjoy right now: using the sun for cooking.

Over a century ago August Mouchot, a French scientist, built a solar cooker. This cooker won a large cash prize for being a practical and better way to cook for soldiers in the field. In our own country, scientists like Samuel Pierpont Langley and Charles Abbot built and used solar cookers fifty years ago. So solar cookery is not as new as we might think. But in general we haven't paid much attention to it because of cheap fuels.

Solar Energy Society

This is a mass-produced solar cooker currently used in India. Such simple reflector stoves can produce about 500 watts at the cooking grill.

Pioneering solar cooking devices were generally bulky, heavy, and expensive to make. Suitable materials were limited and few people knew about putting the sun to work effectively. Technological advances have made solar cookers and other solar devices more available. Lightweight reflective films and plastics are available at reasonable prices. Practical solar equipment can be bought, or home-built. The result is that every day the sun cooks more hamburgers and even turns out full-course dinners.

There are many advantages of cooking with solar energy. Since solar cookers do not require a fire, they are not a fire hazard and can be used in areas closed to fire building. There is no smoke or other pollution from a solar cooker, and no ashes to clean up. Neither is there any wasted time in waiting for a fire to burn down to the proper cooking temperature.

Solar cookery is instructive too. After learning how the sun's energy can do everyday chores it is easier to understand how it can do larger tasks, such as home heating or power generation. The basic principles of heat absorption, sun "tracking," and the "greenhouse effect" become easy to understand. Best of all, using solar energy can be a very enjoyable and exciting experience.

In recent years we have wisely begun to consider the environment and how to protect it. Ecology has become an important discipline. What better way to safeguard and enjoy our world than with the use of solar energy? Here is the natural source that makes life possible by keeping us warm, growing our food, and providing us with fresh water. Why not go the next step and put that available energy to another good use? Solar cookery is an ideal and easy way to do that.

Westinghouse

George A. Towns Elementary School, Atlanta, Georgia. When the picture was taken, this was the largest solar heating and cooling system in operation.

1
SOLAR ENERGY
AND HOW TO USE IT

One of the nicest things about solar energy is that you don't have to be a scientist or an engineer to understand and use it. Just the same, it doesn't hurt to know a few solar basics.

The sun is vital to our lives; without it there would be no gravitation to hold the earth in its orbit, no heat to keep us from freezing, no food to eat, no light to see by. Yet we tend to take all this for granted, seldom recalling the tremendous power in the sun's seemingly gentle rays. For example, in just a few days the sun showers us with as much energy as there is in all the fossil fuels in the entire earth! Thousands of times more solar energy reaches us than we get from all conventional sources, including coal, oil, gas, and nuclear fuels.

The solar radiation falling everyday on a modest-sized house with about 100 square yards of roof area is equivalent to the heat energy in about 175 pounds of coal or about 15 gallons of gasoline. If we convert that solar radiation into electricity at an efficiency of about ten percent, we get about seven kilowatts of electricity while the sun is overhead. A single acre of land in direct sunlight receives almost 4000 horsepower of heat energy; a square mile about 2,500,000 horsepower. It is easy to understand why solar energy as an alternative source is receiving so much attention.

TURNING SUNSHINE INTO HEAT

Our solar oven sometimes gets hotter than 400° F; enough to bake a loaf of bread with a nice brown crust. To produce this heat we must use the simple principles of reflection, concentration, glazing, and absorption. Without using these simple techniques even an outside temperature of 100° F won't do much of a cooking job for us.

A mirror bounces light (and heat) from its reflective surface. Properly arranged, mirrors *concentrate* those sunbeams on the solar oven. Remember how hot your car gets in the summer sun? That's the "greenhouse effect": *glass* lets in solar heat but prevents most of it from escaping. If the car upholstery is black, it gets so hot it is painful to sit on, and a black steering wheel is too hot to handle. This is the process of heat *absorption*. If you have seen a solar collector used for heating water you noticed that it was a deep, non-reflecting black. When we build our solar oven we will make use of this important solar *absorber* principle.

A surface gets hotter when the sun's rays strike it perpendicularly, or head on. Early in the morning or late in the afternoon the glancing rays of the sun are weaker. Thus, solar energy is at a minimum when the sun first rises over the horizon, builds to a maximum at noon when the sun is highest overhead, and then tapers off again to zero at sunset. Fortunately our solar cooking equipment is not hampered by the varying solar output during the day.

The trick is to "track" the sun, by pointing the solar cooker directly at the sun. Even in far northern areas where the sun is low in the sky, we can do almost as well as in southern areas by aiming at the sun.

SOLAR GEOGRAPHY

In Arizona we have an abundance of sunshine. The Yuma area, for example, gets about 4000 hours of sun a year; solar ovens and reflectors work very well in the southwest. But don't be fooled into thinking that if you live somewhere else you can't cook well with solar energy.

Air temperature isn't very important either. Our solar cookers do very well in the winter, even when the air is quite cool. In Flagstaff (7000 ft.) which has very clear air most of the time, a solar oven or reflector does even better than in Phoenix. The same is true for Denver or other high-altitude cities.

The sun shines on just about everyone, and everywhere in the solar belt it is possible to cook with sunshine on a sunny day. We used to think of the solar belt as between the 40th parallels of latitude, but after a visit to a solar conference in Winnipeg we changed our minds. Winnipeg is about 50 degrees north latitude, and solar cookers work there too.

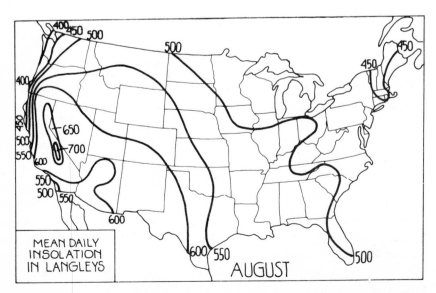

The map shows the amounts of solar energy received in various parts of the country. Note that the areas with the least sunshine still get 75% as much as the sunny southwest.

2
BUILDING THE SOLAR OVEN

The latest in our series of solar ovens is much simpler to build than earlier models. Constructed of plywood, ordinary window glass, and any of a variety of reflective materials, the oven can be completed in a short time.

Check the list of supplies and get together the materials you will need for the oven. Perhaps you have scraps of plywood large enough for the box; maybe even an old window pane that will do for the glass door. Reflectors may be made from corrugated cardboard cut from cartons if you don't want to buy new cardboard. Heavy-duty aluminum foil (the kind you wrap a turkey in for broiling) will serve for reflective material to bounce additional heat into the oven, but aluminized mylar sheets are more durable.

Read through the directions before you start construction, making certain that you have all the materials and that you understand the process.

List of Supplies Needed for Construction of Solar Oven
1 pc. plywood 3/4" x 16-1/2" x 17-1/4" (sides)
1 pc. plywood 3/4" x 16-1/2" x 18" (top & bottom)
1 pc. plywood 3/4" x 19-1/2" x 17-1/4" (back)
1 pc. plywood 3/4" x 6" x 8" (stairstep)
8 sq. ft. 1" pressed fiberglas insulation
1 pc. double-strength window glass 18-7/8" x 18-7/8"
4 pcs. wood strips 1/8" x 3/8" x 20"
8 pcs. 16-guage aluminum or iron 1" x 4" (attachment angles)
4 pcs. cardboard, masonite, or aluminum sheet 18" x 18"
1 roll double-strength aluminum foil 18" wide
1 pc. wooden drawer knob 1", and attaching screw
1 fiber washer to fit drawer knob attaching screw
30 finishing nails 2" long
12 big-headed roofing nails 1½" long
8 round-headed wood screws 5/8", #10
8 round-headed bolts ½", #10
8 nuts #10
8 washers 1", 3/16" hole
1 oven rack 8" x 12"
2 pcs. wood dowel 1/2", 3" long
2 pcs. brass rod 1/8", 15" long
1 sheet sandpaper
1 can non-toxic flat black paint

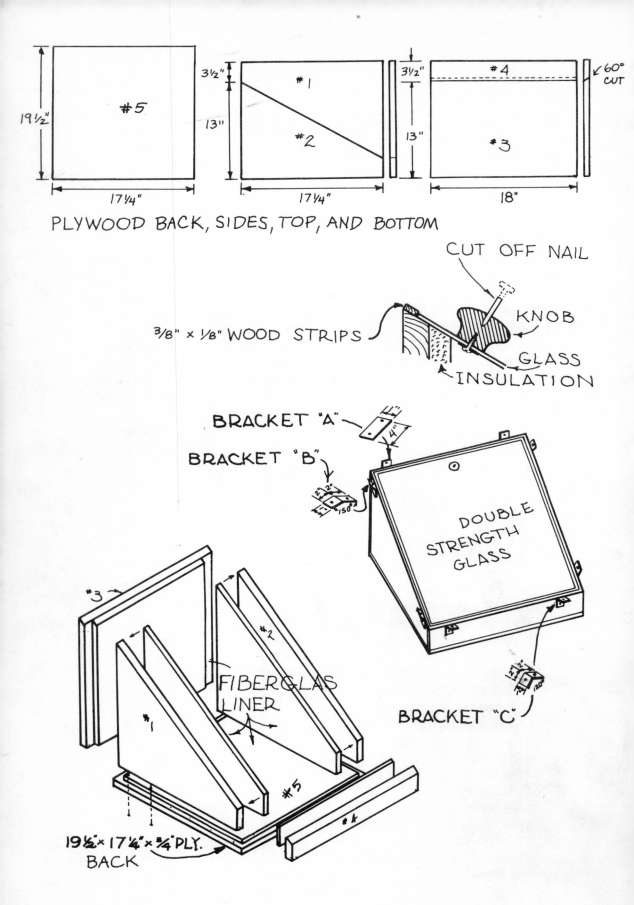

#5

19½"

17¼"

3½"

#1

13"

#2

17¼"

3½"

#4

13"

#3

18"

60° CUT

PLYWOOD BACK, SIDES, TOP, AND BOTTOM

CUT OFF NAIL

KNOB

GLASS

INSULATION

3/8" × 1/8" WOOD STRIPS

BRACKET "A"

BRACKET "B"

DOUBLE STRENGTH GLASS

BRACKET "C"

#3

#2

FIBERGLAS LINER

#1

#5

#4

19½" × 17¼" × ¾" PLY. BACK

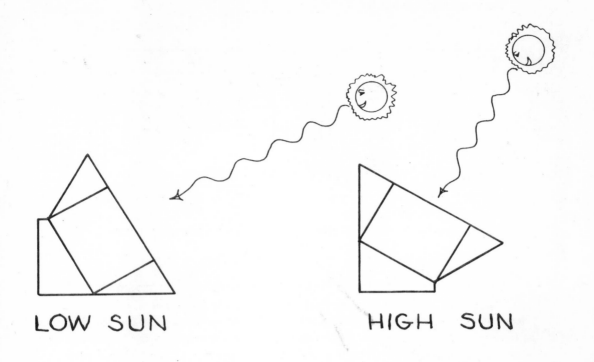

LOW SUN

HIGH SUN

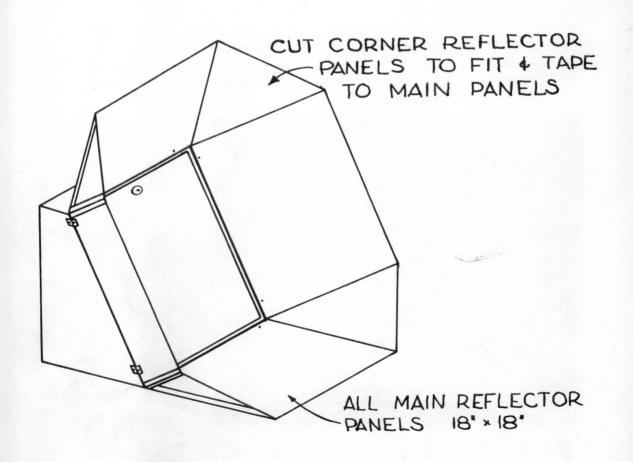

CUT CORNER REFLECTOR
PANELS TO FIT & TAPE
TO MAIN PANELS

ALL MAIN REFLECTOR
PANELS 18" x 18"

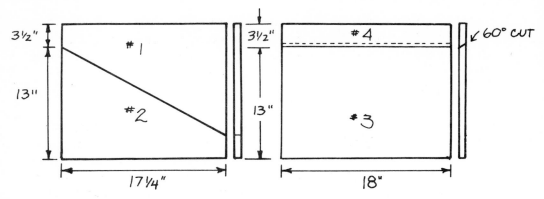

LAYOUT FOR CUTTING THE SIDES, TOP, AND BOTTOM OF OVEN

THE OVEN BOX

Make the body of the oven first. Note that the plans show a rectangle from which you cut both side pieces, and another rectangle for the end pieces. This saves wood and also makes construction easier. A table saw will make nice straight cuts, but if you don't have one, don't worry. Our oven was constructed entirely with hand tools.

sides — parts 1 and 2

Cut the rectangle that will form the sides. Make sure to get the dimensions accurate so that the parts will fit together neatly. (You can have this done at the lumber yard.) Now mark a line in the proper place to divide the smaller rectangle into the two side pieces. Saw right on the line, using power

Dan using the clamped board guide to help saw the sides accurately.

tools if available. If not, clamp a straight board onto the plywood just on the pencil line. Hold the saw next to the guide and saw straight up and down. When you have completed the cut, the two pieces should match. Set them aside while you work on the top and bottom.

top and bottom — parts 3 and 4

We used a simple method to save work in making the top and bottom pieces from the larger rectangle shown in the plans. Glue and nail the sides to the uncut piece, as shown in the photo. We put glue on one side, stood on the uncut top and bottom piece and held the side piece in place carefully, lining up the edges at the back of the oven. Nail with 2'' finishing nails. Then do the same for the other side piece.

With both sides nailed to the uncut piece (it will stick out as shown in photo) draw guide lines on both sides so it will be easy to saw accurately. Now carefully saw, frequently checking to see that you are following the guide lines. Take your time and make an accurate cut. The piece you have cut off should then fit neatly between the sides to form the top.

back — part 5

Now you are ready to glue and nail on the oven back. Apply glue and carefully nail the back to the already assembled sides, bottom, and top. Use 2'' finishing nails. Keep all edges even so that the oven is square and true, and smooth it with sand paper so that the glass cover will lie flat on the open face.

Left - The piece cut from the rectangle will become the oven top. Note the strip of wood holding sides together. *Right* - The completed oven box. Use wood filler where necessary to close up any gaps.

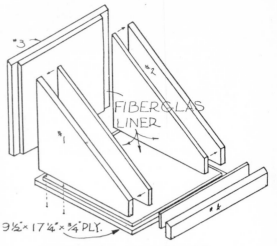

ASSEMBLY OF THE OVEN BOX
AND FIBERGLAS LINER

Left - Trim the aluminum part of the insulation after securing with roofing nails, so that it can be easily stapled to oven box.

INSULATION

If we were content with a temperature of about 250° or a little higher, we could stop right here. Instead, lets add an inch of fiberglass insulation so that the oven will get really hot. We used insulation bought at an air conditioning supply house. It is pressed fiberglass, faced on one side with tough aluminum foil. Cost is low, and the material is easy to cut for fitting into the oven. Use a knife or saw.

Plan all the cuts so that the aluminum side of the insulation will be showing in the oven, and not up against the plywood walls. Fit the side pieces first. Trim one and use it as a pattern for the other — being careful to make them opposite so you get the aluminum foil on the correct side. We tacked the insulation in place with the roofing nails. Remember the insulation is soft, so don't drive the nail in below the surface of the foil. Fit the top and bottom pieces and nail into place. Then cut a piece for the back, push it into place, and nail.

Remember our discussion on a good solar energy absorber? Right now the shiny aluminum surface makes a good reflector instead. So we will paint it dull black. You can brush the paint on, or use a spray can. Be sure to buy a paint labeled "non-toxic."

GLASS DOOR

The opening of your oven should measure 18" square. The glass cover overlaps 3/8" all around, thus the glass cover is 18 3/4" square. Have this cut at the glass shop unless you are experienced in working with glass. Use

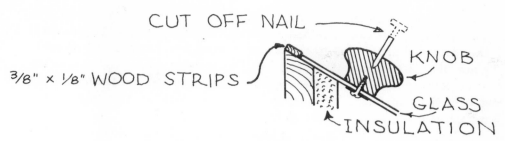

CUT OFF NAIL

3/8" × 1/8" WOOD STRIPS

KNOB

GLASS

INSULATION

DETAIL OF OVEN DOOR HANDLE

double-strength window glass. Have the edges sanded for safety and also have a 3/16" hole drilled on one side. The hole should be 2" from the edge and centered, as shown on the plans.

The small hole in the glass is for attaching the wooden knob that will be the handle for opening and closing the oven door. We bought a 1" wooden knob and attaching screw for 13¢, and it works fine. You may have to cut the end of the screw off with a hacksaw since the glass is much thinner than the wood which the knob would usually be attached to.

Also drill a small hole in the front center of the knob, as shown in the plans. This should be a tight fit for a short length of nail from which the head has been removed. We inserted the nail by squeezing it and the knob in a vise. The nail should protrude from the front of the knob about 3/4". This is a simple sun-tracking device. Now assemble the knob to the glass, using a fiber washer between the screw and the glass to guard against cracks.

To retain the glass cover on the front of the oven add wood strips all around, as shown in the plans and photo. To simplify this task, we bought strips of balsa wood from as model airplane shop. They were 1/8" x 3/8" x 36". We bought three and used cut-offs to piece together for the fourth side. If you want, you can substitute basswood, pine, or another kind of wood.

The wood strips are being glued to the oven face. The pins hold the strips in place while the glue dries.

As shown in the photo, block up the oven with the front face level. Lay the glass on it, with an equal distance from the glass edges to the outside of the box. Now apply glue to the strips of wood and carefully lay them in place, not quite touching the glass. Don't let the glue run out from under the wood strips and touch the glass as this may cause you a little extra work getting the glass loose. Use quick-drying glue for this job. You may want to pin the strips in place until the glue is completely dry.

Your oven will now work. In fact, this was all that early solar cooks used. On a good bright day our oven will reach 250° without attached reflector panels. This will do a great deal of cooking, but there are times when 250° just isn't enough. So let's make the shiny reflectors that bounce more solar energy into the oven.

REFLECTORS

The reflectors can be made several different ways. We've had good results using reflectors made from ½'' urethane foam with aluminum foil backing. This material (used for home insulation) is very light and not very expensive. In fact, a 4' x 8' sheet costs about $8, and makes a lot of reflectors. Our present oven has reflectors of polished sheet aluminum. We have also used aluminized mylar glues to thin masonite, or other suitable backing material. Just about anything will work as long as you keep it flat, smooth, and shiny. With thin material like sheet aluminum you can make the reflectors fold on hinges. This protects the glass cover while it is not in use and also makes the oven easily portable.

Perhaps the simplest method is to cut out 18'' squares of corrugated cardboard and glue aluminum foil to them. If you do a smooth job, these will work almost as well as glass mirrors, and they are feather-light, cheap, and easily replaced.

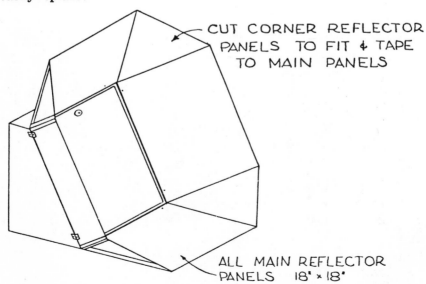

CUT CORNER REFLECTOR PANELS TO FIT & TAPE TO MAIN PANELS

ALL MAIN REFLECTOR PANELS 18' × 18'

REFLECTOR PANELS ATTACHED AND TAPED

We have had the best results by using a double layer of cardboard instead of a single sheet. This keeps the cardboard from warping as it tends to do when it gets damp or warm. Apply a coating of glue (rubber cement, white glue, or contact cement) to the cardboard squares. Then press them together and lay them on a flat surface with a moderate weight holding them together until dry. (Remember, you will need eight 18'' squares if you use the double-layer method.)

With the cardboard squares dry and flat, you are ready to apply the aluminum. Be sure to use double-strength foil, in an 18'' roll. It is possible to use thinner foil, but heavy-duty foil is so much easier to use it is worth the slight additional cost.

We find it easier to apply glue to the cardboard and then place the carboard on the foil, rather than doing it the other way. There is less chance of wrinkling the foil this way. Don't trim the foil until it is glued to the cardboard, and use a razor blade or sharp knife. Weight the cardboard and aluminum foil while they dry.

ATTACHMENT ANGLES

Since light bounces off a mirror at the same angle it strikes it, we can attach a reflector the same size as the opening in our oven box and reflect all the light striking it into that opening. But this is so only if we keep the reflector at an angle of 120° from the glass cover, as shown on the plans. The way the box is cut, the top and bottom reflectors require different angle attachments than the sides. So make sure you have all the angles bent correctly or you will be wasting solar energy and not cooking as well as you could.

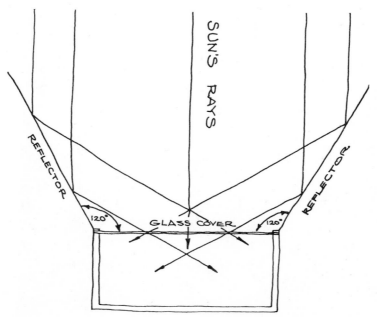

HOW THE REFLECTORS WORK

We had six of the eight angles bent at a sheet metal shop for accuracy and to save time. Aluminum is excellent; it should be 1/16'' thick and not soft. If you cannot find aluminum, galvanized or black iron will do. Use 16 guage metal. The angles are made from blanks 1'' x 4'' which are bent in the center of the 4'' dimension. Because of the shape of the oven box, two fittings are left flat; two are bent to an open angle of 150°, and four are 120°. Make sure that the angles are exact so that each reflector will make the proper angle with the glass cover of your oven.

Drill 3/16'' holes in both ends of each attachment fitting as shown on the plans. Clean the burrs from these holes with a slightly larger drill held in the hand, or with a knife blade you don't care too much about. Now you can attach the angles to the oven box. Hold an angle in place and line up its free leg with the face of the oven as shown on the plan. Mark through the hole onto the plywood for the location of the screw hole. To speed up the process, go ahead and mark all the holes now and do all the drilling at once.

It will help to center punch the hole locations before drilling to help you drill accurately. It will also help if you wrap a short piece of tape around the drill so you won't drill completely through the 3/4'' plywood. About 5/8'' deep is enough. Use #10 screws, 5/8'' long. These should be round headed wood screws. Tighten the angles in place, and you are now ready to install the reflector panels on the angles.

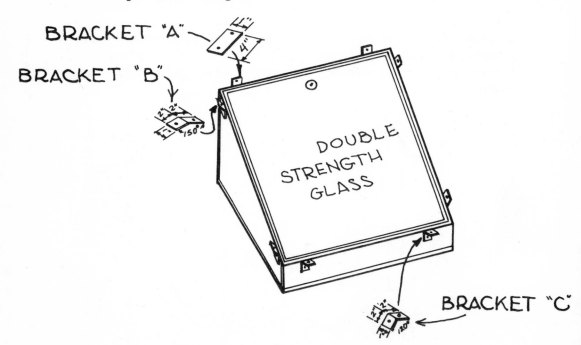

DETAIL OF REFLECTOR MOUNTING BRACKETS

Hold a reflector panel in place (with the aluminum foil facing the glass) just clearing the glass cover. Mark the panel very carefully with a pencil through the hole in the attaching angle. Again you may want to use the mass production technique and mark all your panels at once.

We found the most accurate way to put the holes in the cardboard was to carefully force a punch or ice pick through the small pencil-marked circles. Then run the 3/16" drill through the punched hole. When you have drilled eight holes you are ready to mount the reflectors to the oven and see how hot your solar oven will get.

The reflectors are attached to the angles with #10 nuts and bolts, and a 1" washer under the bolt head on the reflector side. This large washer keeps the bolt from pulling through the soft cardboard. Attach all four reflectors, tightening the bolts snugly with screw driver and pliers.

If you have been keeping track of how much additional sunshine the reflectors capture, you know that you are now doubling the amount of solar energy going into the oven, and its temperature will really soar. You can add a bit more heat by filling in the corners as shown in the plans and photos. Cut four cardboard/foil triangles to fit into the gap. Tape them neatly in place with masking tape or duct tape. Now your oven should reach 400° on good days, and that will take care of just about anything you want to cook.

The completed reflector oven with the triangles fitted into the corners.

The ultimate, of course, is to put hinges on the reflectors so that it takes only a couple of minutes to fold up for easy carrying. We use sheet aluminum reflectors on our present oven, attached to the oven body by lengths of piano hinge. The hinge is riveted to the aluminum reflectors and wood screwed to the plywood box. All we have to do is remove the tape holding the reflectors together, take out two nuts and bolts (from the top reflector) and the job is done. Of course we still use the attaching angles to keep the reflectors at the correct angle.

The reflectors won't close down flat over the knob on the glass door, so we just take the door off, turn it over, and put it back on. That leaves a nearly flat surface instead of the knob and the reflectors lie down smoothly.

Folding up the solar oven for carrying.

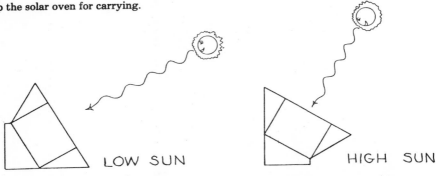

USING THE LOW AND HIGH POSITIONS OF THE SOLAR OVEN

ANGLE ADJUSTER

Our first solar oven had its glass cover angled at 45°. But somewhere along the way we realized that if we made it 30° instead, we could use the oven in two positions and thus be aiming at the sun more accurately for a longer part of the day. As the sketches show, for early morning and late afternoon cooking, you can flop the oven to another position. This makes it look lower in the sky, where the sun is at these times. We call this our "high-sun," "low-sun feature," and it really helps.

Even this improvement doesn't guarantee perfect aiming all day long, of course. So for those awkward, in-between times we give you the angle adjuster (idea from Sam Erwin) with which you can easily aim so exactly that you can make the sun's shadow disappear on the tracking knob. You can reach hot enough temperatures to brown the meringue on a lemon pie or do other high-temperature baking. As shown in the photo, raise the oven with one hand until it is aimed where you want it, then slide the stairstep in to hold it there. Build the angle adjuster as shown in the plans, using 3/4" plywood.

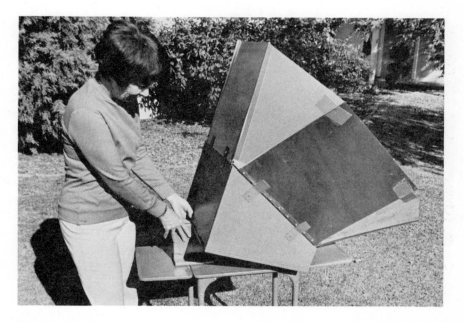

Beth using the angle adjuster to aim the oven at the sun. Note how the reflector panels are taped together.

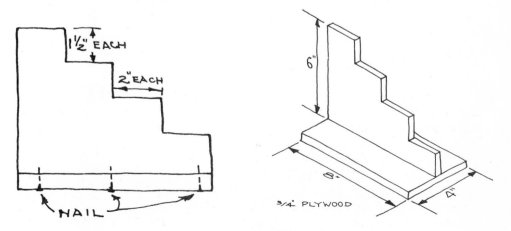

SOLAR OVEN ANGLE ADJUSTER

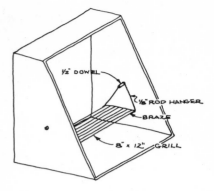

SWINGING OVEN RACK

OVEN RACK

We thought at first that we had all our problems solved, until a casserole ran out of its tipped dish. So we added another feature: a swinging oven rack that keeps the pan level no matter what the oven does.

Starting with a rack bought in the household goods department, we had the sheetmetal man add wire hangers at each end, as shown in the sketch. We used iron at first but soon learned that it rusts quickly in the high oven temperatures. So we substituted brass rod and have had no further trouble.

The hangers fit over short lengths of 1/2'' wood dowel glued into 1/2'' holes drilled through the sides of the oven as shown. Using this handy accessory you can be sure a pie won't slop over or a loaf of bread won't come out looking like it was baked on the side of a hill.

A little paint really dresses up the solar oven. Pick your favorite color and either spray or brush the outside of your creation a gleaming "solar yellow," "fire red," "flame orange," or whatever suits your taste. We painted the angle adjuster too. None of the colors will do anything for the temperature inside but will make your oven much more attractive. Ours is orange and we like it.

USING THE SOLAR OVEN

Your solar oven is now ready to test. Pick a sunny spot in the patio or backyard (or the front yard, if you like) and set up. The oven will work well right on the ground, or you can put it on a small table for more convenience. In either case, have it as level as possible. We have our oven on an old typewriter table on wheels and that works very well.

We get the most sunlight into the oven by pointing it as directly at the sun as possible. The nail we put into the knob on the glass door is the sun-tracker that lets you aim the oven right at the sun. Aim your oven at the sun

The finger is pointing to the shadow on the knob. Adjust the oven until the shadow disappears; the solar oven will then be pointing directly at the sun.

as best you can, and then check the shadow on the knob. (You'll see several faint shadows, but use the dark one.) Adjust the oven until you make the shadow vanish. It's that simple.

Because your oven will get very hot, the black paint on the inside will give off fumes and smell for a while. So set the oven out in bright sun and keep it focused to burn off this paint. We always do this for a few days with a new oven and then we never get any paint smell in the food. You may find that a film is deposited on the inside of the glass. Wipe this off from time to time until the glass stays clean. Now you can go ahead and start cooking with the solar oven.

Loading food into the oven is easy. Remove the glass door so you can put the food in. Then replace the cover and start cooking. An inexpensive oven thermometer should be standard equipment. This will give you an idea of cooking temperature, and also impress your friends who won't otherwise believe that a solar oven can reach 445°.

THE PORTABLE SOLAR OVEN

For around home it is easy just to leave the oven set up all the time. It is even a great conversation piece. Put some kind of cover over it to keep dust from the glass door and you won't have to clean it as often. Sooner or later, though, you will want to take the oven on a picnic or even a camping trip. In assembled form it is rather bulky, so just remove the nuts and bolts and stack the reflectors against the glass door for a compact solar oven for traveling. We installed a nice carrying handle on ours and this makes it even simpler to transport.

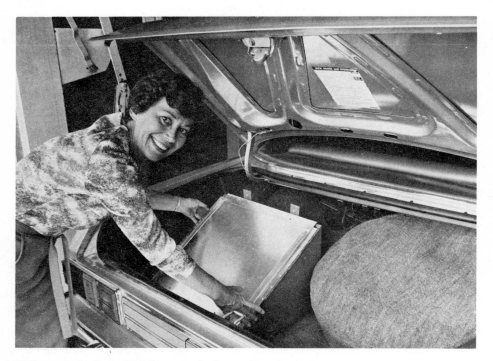

Beth can easily fit the folded-up oven in the small trunk of a compact car.

3
BUILDING THE
SOLAR HOT PLATE

The solar oven handles a great variety of baked dishes. But how about coffee or hot chocolate? Or bacon and eggs, hot cakes, or even a juicy steak? For this kind of cooking we need much higher temperatures, focused onto a much smaller cooking area. In short, we need a solar hot plate.

Years ago we heard about a reflector stove made of cardboard, by a man named Max Flindt, and the idea appealed to us. Cardboard is inexpensive, easy to use, and lightweight. So we tried one and it worked very well. The solar hot plate plans in this book are the latest in a long line of different designs, sizes, and shapes. We think it is the best.

Our first reflector cooker was a giant, 48" in diameter. It cooked well but it was difficult to store and almost impossible to take anywhere unless we had a pickup truck. After several generations of development, we realized that if the reflector was square instead of round it could be smaller in overall dimensions and still generate as much heat. This reflector stove is only 32" square but does an excellent cooking job.

List of Supplies Needed for Construction of Solar Hot Plate

3 pcs. cardboard 1/8" x 4' x 8' (reflector box and cover)
1 pc. pipe flange 3/4"
1 pc. pipe nipple 3/4", 4" long
1 pc. aluminum tubing 3/4", 24" long
8 sq. ft. double-strength aluminum foil or aluminized mylar*
1 iron lampshade ring 5-1/2"
1 pc. iron rod 1/8", 6" long
1 pc. threaded iron rod 3/16", 2-1/2" long
1 pc. wood 1" x 2" x 35"
1 bolt 3/16", 1-1/2" long
3 nuts 3/16"
1 sheet poster board
1 finishing nail
1 pc. heavy string 12"

*Available from Edmund Scientific, Barrington, NJ 08007

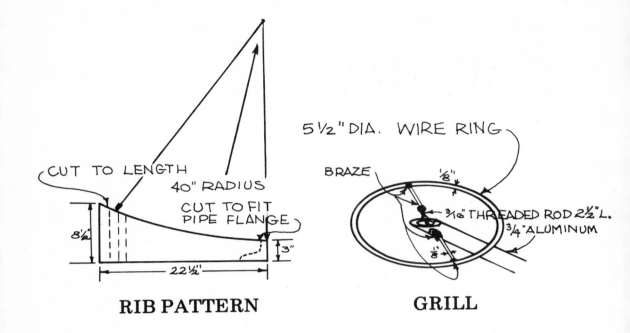

RIB PATTERN

CUT TO LENGTH
40" RADIUS
CUT TO FIT PIPE FLANGE
8½"
3"
22½"

GRILL

5½" DIA. WIRE RING
BRAZE
⅛"
³⁄₁₆" THREADED ROD 2½" L.
¾" ALUMINUM
⅛"

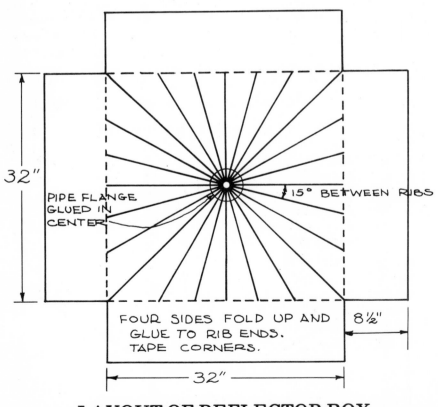

32"
PIPE FLANGE GLUED IN CENTER
15° BETWEEN RIBS
FOUR SIDES FOLD UP AND GLUE TO RIB ENDS. TAPE CORNERS.
8½"
32"

LAYOUT OF REFLECTOR BOX

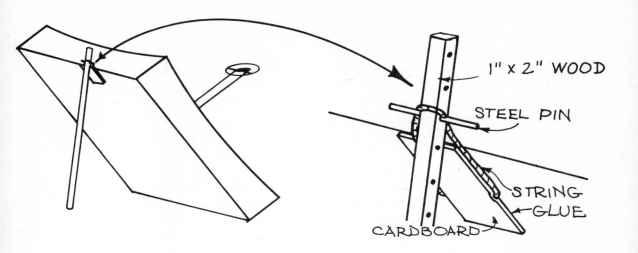

REFLECTOR COOKER SUPPORT

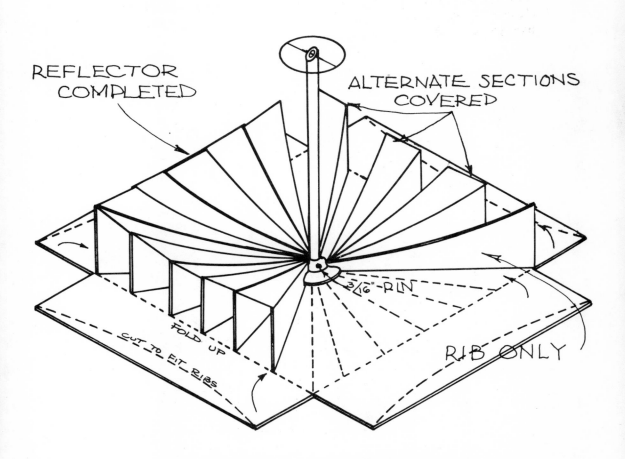

HOT PLATE ASSEMBLY

HOW THE SOLAR HOT PLATE WORKS

You have probably used a magnifying glass to burn wood or leaves. A curved mirror does about the same thing, concentrating all the sunlight that strikes it into a tiny, very hot spot. Solar furnaces can be made in this way, and old searchlight mirrors are often put to such use. The parabolic curve of the mirror results in almost perfect concentration and temperatures of several thousand degrees. This would burn holes in a frying pan, so we neither need nor want that kind of mirror.

For simplicity we use a circular curve rather than a parabola. It is much easier to draw. We also form our mirror with a series of wedge-shaped pieces of flat material instead of trying to mould them into a compound curve. This makes the task a lot easier, and results in a hot spot about 6" square instead of a pinpoint. We estimate its temperature at about 500° F, since a piece of newspaper held at the focal point bursts into flame instantly.

While the solar hot plate is easy to build (we build them and are not very skilled craftsmen) it does take some patience and care to build it correctly. Careless or sloppy work will result in a cooker that won't get as hot as you'd like. So work slowly and accurately.

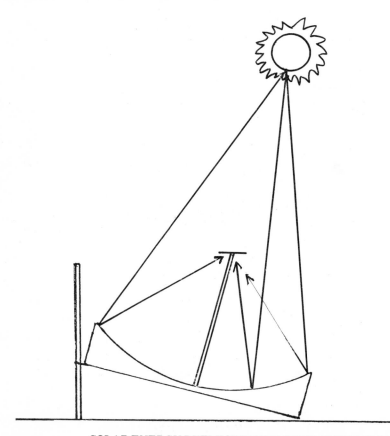

SOLAR ENERGY REFLECTING TO COOKER HOT SPOT

CARDBOARD BASE

Start by reading the directions and assembling the materials called for in the list of materials. You can buy 4' x 8' sheets of cardboard at a paper box factory. Or you can scrounge up used cardboard in sizes big enough for the cooker. Buy the aluminum tubing at the hardward store or search out bargains at a scrap metal place. Maybe you are lucky enough to have material on hand.

Cut out a base piece of cardboard as shown in the drawings. Notch the corners and draw the lines that locate the ribs, making sure they intersect right at the center of the square. Draw the two diagonal lines first. Next find the midpoint of each side piece, and draw two more lines connecting them. Now, with a protractor, divide each of the resulting 45° angles into three equal 15° angles. Twenty-four ribs times 15° equals 360° or a full circle. Draw all these lines, making sure they cross the center of the square.

Now turn the cardboard over and draw lines connecting the points of the corner notches. Very carefully cut through just one layer of cardboard using a straightedge so the cut will be accurate. What you want to do is make it easy to bend the sides up when we reach that point in the construction, so don't cut all the way through.

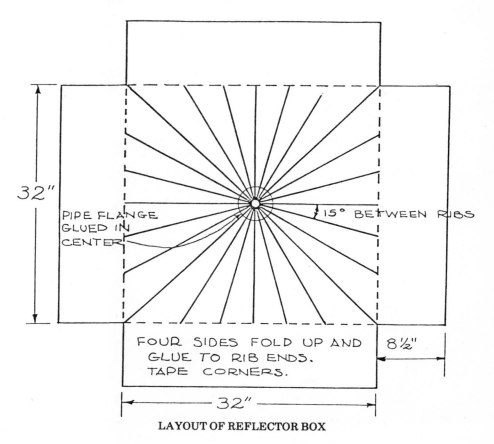

LAYOUT OF REFLECTOR BOX

DETAIL OF GRILL MOUNT

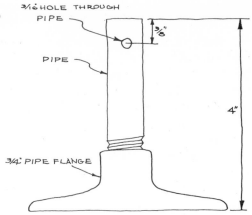

FLANGE ASSEMBLY

An important part of the cooker assembly is the flange that will support the cooking grill. Screw the 3/4'' pipe nipple tightly into the 3/4'' flange. Set the flange on a flat surface and measure up 4''. Mark the pipe and then either cut off the excess with a hacksaw, or have it done at the sheet metal shop. File the end smooth and clean out the inside of pipe so that the aluminum tubing will slide in easily. Now drill the 3/16'' hole through the pipe as shown in the sketch.

The flange must be at the exact center of the reflector, so apply glue liberally to its bottom surface and set it right over the intersection of the lines marking the ribs. Make sure glue runs up out of the holes in the flange so that it will stick tightly to the cardboard.

The reflector bottom has been marked for rib location and the sides have been trimmed. Note that the grill mounting flange has been secured with plenty of glue.

LAYOUT OF PATTERN FOR LONGEST RIB

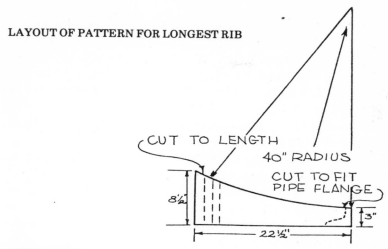

CUT TO LENGTH

40" RADIUS

CUT TO FIT
PIPE FLANGE

8½"

3"

22½"

MAKING THE RIBS

First you will need a pattern for cutting ribs from the second cardboard sheet. You can make this pattern from cardboard too, and this is perhaps the easiest way to do it. As shown on the drawing, draw a 40" radius beginning at a point 3" from the end of the cardboard sheet and right at its edge. Arrange the curve so that you will be cutting across the corrugations and not along them as this makes a much better cut.

Some particular craftsmen make a rib pattern of metal. Aluminum is a good choice because it is easy to cut. With such a pattern, it is easy to cut right along its edge with a knife or razor blade. However you make your pattern, cut it out carefully. On cardboard, use a sharp knife, linoleum cutter, razor blade, or even a small hand saw. If necessary, sandpaper the pattern so it is smooth and right on the line.

The master rib pattern is being made using a long strip of wood with a pencil inserted in a hole at the proper length.

Since the ribs cannot reach to the center of the circle because the flange is in the way, cut off an amount half the diameter of the flange from the 3'' end of the rib pattern. Trim a bit more from the bottom so the pattern clears the base of the flange. Now place it on the cardboard square, snug against the flange, and mark the end of the longest, or diagonal rib. Make sure you get a vertical line here, and trim the pattern. Mark four ribs on the cardboard, remembering to arrange the cuts across the corrugations. Cut these out carefully and set aside.

Now place the long rib pattern on the next shortest line on the base piece, with its small end right up against the flange. Make a vertical pencil line on the pattern to mark the end of the next shortest rib and trim off the excess material with a razor blade or sharp knife. Now you have a pattern for another rib. Use it to mark out eight ribs. Cut these ribs out as you did the others and set them aside.

Move your pattern to the next shortest rib and again mark the end. Trim off the excess and use the new pattern to mark out eight more ribs. After these are cut out, you can move the pattern to the last rib and trim it off. There are only four of these so don't make too many. You should now have 24 ribs in all.

Remember our caution about accuracy. Check the ribs against each other by setting them on a flat surface and holding the small ends even. The curves should match; if they don't the reflective material won't accurately focus the sun's rays on the grill. If necessary, do some more trimming or sanding so that the ribs all have the same curve.

The pattern has been traced on cardboard blanks which are all the same size. The pieces will be glued together so that the curves can be cut all at once.

One way to get very accurate ribs is to cut out two dozen rough blanks of cardboard large enough so that you can trace the pattern on a blank. Glue all the blanks in a stack, putting glue outside the pattern so that the ribs will come apart later. Now cut the ribs on a bandsaw and all the ribs are exactly the same.

RIB ASSEMBLY

We used model airplane glue (any quick-drying cement will do) so that we didn't have to hold the ribs in place very long. Just put a spot of glue every 6″ or so along the lines on the cardboard base and hold the proper rib in place until the glue has set. Make sure that the base piece is on a flat surface and does not curl up. You may want to weight it with bricks, paint cans, or something else to keep it flat until you get enough ribs in place. When all the ribs are glued in place, let them dry long enough for full strength. Overnight is best if you have that much patience.

Then it is time to bend up the sides of the box and mark the top edges of the ribs so you can trim the sides in the gentle curve shown on the drawing and photos. This can be done by laying a strip of thin wood, which will bow, so that it touches all the points you have marked. Trim off the excess with a knife or linoleum cutter and prop one side up at a time for gluing. Use about two big drops of glue on each side of each rib. When all four box sides are glued in place, prop the box almost vertical against a wall and add more

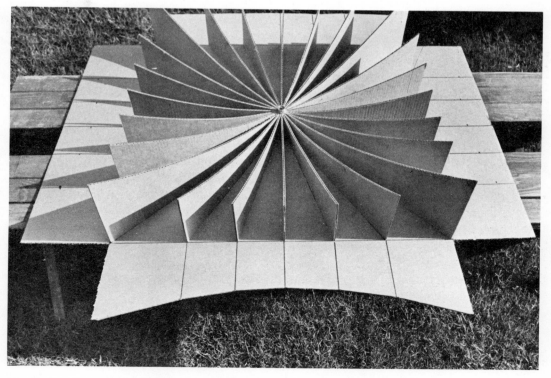

The ribs have been glued to the box and one side is trimmed and ready to be glued in place.

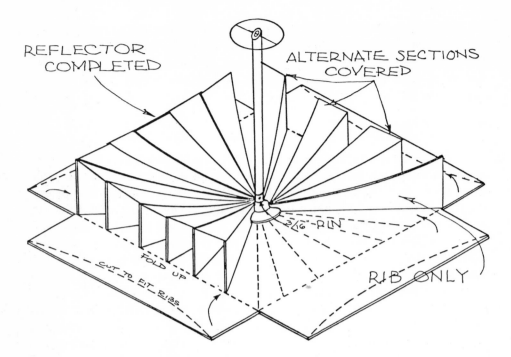

glue, especially at the corners and at the center where the ribs touch the flange. Let glue dry, turn box 90° and add more glue. Repeat until all joints are glued. This will make it sturdy enough to survive an occasional hard knock.

THE MIRROR FINISH

You have completed the skeleton of your reflector. There are several ways to make the mirror finish. Double-strength aluminin foil can be glued to poster board to make a durable, easily worked reflector material. Or you can use sheets of aluminized Mylar (from Edmund Scientific Corporation) and glue these to the poster board. The second method is easiest and will make the smoothest job. If you do use aluminum foil, takes lots of care to get it smooth, with no wrinkles. Otherwise, the mirror will not concentrate solar energy as well and your solar hot plate may only get warm!

Don't try to apply aluminum foil, or even the Edmund Mylar material, directly to the cardboard ribs. It will not be smooth enough (especially the aluminum foil). Be sure to glue the foil to sturdy poster board first. We used rubber cement.

Make a pattern from poster board of the longest triangle you will need. It should completely cover two ribs. Mark four of these triangles on the foil-posterboard and cut them out. Then turn the pattern over and mark four "opposite-hand" wedges. There are three different sizes of triangles, so repeat this procedure twice. You should now have all 24 triangles cut out, and are ready to start making the big curved mirror.

The completed reflector box has a circle of foil glued to the box where the narrow triangle ends meet. Note that the circle fits around the flange.

The easiest way is to cover every other opening first, as shown in the drawing. Use quick-drying cement, and apply it to the edges of the back side of one triangle. Put glue only where it will contact the ribs. Put the triangle in place, and hold it down firmly while the glue dries. Start with any triangle and do every other one, leaving an opening to be filled in the next step of construction. This makes each section of reflector focus its sun's rays accurately on the grill. When the glue has dried, you can start filling in the open spaces.

You don't need to be too fussy in fitting the narrow ends up against the flange because we'll add a circle of foil at the center, as shown in the illustrations. Mark a 4" circle on a piece of foil glued to posterboard and cut it out carefully. Also cut out a smaller round hole in the center, to fit over the pipe. Glue to the flange and reflector.

When the glue is well dried, turn the box over and apply masking tape to the outside joints. Except for a coat or two of whatever color paint or enamel you prefer, the reflector inself is complete, unless you want to make a cardboard cover for it as shown in the photograph on the next page. The cover is made like you made the box itself. Be sure to make it big enough to slip over the reflector.

The completed cover fits snugly over the reflector box. Note how the reflector support holds up the box.

REFLECTOR SUPPORT

The 35" x 1" x 2" piece of wood is used to prop the reflector up at different angles to face the sun. Mark 12 holes on the 1" side, as shown in the drawing. Start 1½" from the end, and make the holes 1½" apart. Drill them through the wood, using a drill that will just let a finishing nail fit snugly through. By positioning the nail in different holes you will be able to support the reflector at any desired angle.

Make a loop from the 12" length of string and attach it to the underside of the reflector box, as shown in the detail drawing. A rectangle of cardboard about 2" x 6" is glued on over the string to hold it in place. Now you can slip the support stick through the loop of string.

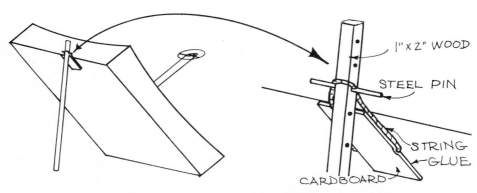

1" x 2" WOOD

STEEL PIN

STRING

GLUE

CARDBOARD

CONSTRUCTION OF REFLECTOR SUPPORT

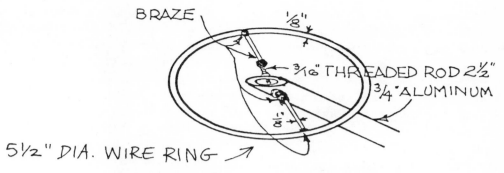

BRAZE

⅛"

³⁄₁₆" THREADED ROD 2½"

¾" ALUMINUM

⅛"

5½" DIA. WIRE RING ↗

CONSTRUCTION OF HOT PLATE GRILL

THE HOT PLATE

Slip one end of the 3/4" aluminum tubing into the flange in the center of the reflector. It will be loose so wrap masking tape around the tubing until it is a snug fit.

Because of the 40" radius curve of the ribs, the focal length of your reflector should be about 20". On ours we check to make sure. To check, insert the aluminum tubing in the flange and set up the reflector so that there is no shadow from the tubing. This means you are pointing directly at the sun. Now take a piece of wrapping paper about a foot square and cut a hole in the center of it large enough to slide easily over the aluminum tubing. Holding it at the edges, slide the paper onto the tubing and watch the bright, square spot that should be formed by your reflector. Move the paper back and forth until that spot is the smallest you can make it: this will be the focal point of your particular stove. Make a mark on the tubing being careful not to burn yourself on the hot metal. Move it out of the sun and when it is cool cut it to that length, which should be about 20". Now we are ready to install the grill.

The aluminum tube, with the grill mounted on one end, has been fitted into the pipe flange.

We bought a 5½" diameter iron ring at the hobby shop. It is normally used in making lamp shades, but it is just right for our hot plate grill. Drill a 3/16" hole in the end of the 3/4" aluminum tubing as shown and insert the length of 3/16" threaded rod. Twist on a 3/16" nut on each side, and cut the two short pieces of plain 1/8" rod as shown on the drawing. If you are not that much of a metal worker, have the brazing done at the local sheetmetal shop. Take along the drawing so they will know what you need. (We had ours done that way.) Just be sure only one nut is brazed to the threaded rod. The other is left free so that it can be used to tighten the grill in a horizontal position no matter what angle your reflector cooker must be tipped to face the sun.

You will notice that the end of the aluminum tubing sticks up slightly above the surface of the grill. File off the excess at an angle, as shown in the detail sketch. Now pots and pans will sit level on the grill.

It is time to attach the lower end of the aluminum tubing to the flange so that the grill will not twist and dump the coffee pot or frying pan. There are already holes in the flange assembly. Prop the cooker up on its support in a shady place so the sun won't be a problem. Level the grill (use a level if you have one, your good eyesight if you haven't) and hold it in place.

With a short, sharp pencil, reach through the holes in the flange and mark onto the aluminum tubing. Remove the tubing, be sure you have two marks, and then center punch the very center of the penciled circles. Drill 3/16" holes, one from each side. Then carefully run the drill through the tubing. Re-insert the aluminum tubing in the flange and see if a 3/16" bolt will go in. If not, you may have to enlarge the holes in the tubing a bit with a slightly larger drill or a round file. Slide the bolt into place, tighten the nut, and you are about ready to use the grill.

The hot spot is *very* hot and you will want to keep your hands out of that area. So how are you going to tighten the grill in the level position? What we do is stand in front of the cooker to shade most of it and thus cut down on the heat. Another way to do it is to turn the cooker away from the sun, keeping it at the proper tilt, and then tighten up the grill. The hot spot is very bright too, so it's a good idea to wear dark glasses for comfort while working with the solar hot plate.

COOKING WITH SUNSHINE

The solar hot plate differs from the kitchen range. It is lots more fun, for one thing. It also uses a moving source of heat, which makes cooking more interesting. As the sun moves, so does the focal point of your hot plate. Ideally, the reflector should point right at the sun (you can tell this from the shadow of the grill) but you don't have to stand by every minute to move it. For some cooking tasks you can position the hot plate once and forget it. For others, you may want to move it every 15 minutes or so to speed up the process. One helpful trick is to "lead" the sun a little bit. With experience you will learn how fast the shadow of the grill moves across the reflector. To get the most heat, aim the cooker enough ahead of the sun so that it will be aimed right at the sun about midway through the cooking period. This will guarantee the fastest cooking time if you don't want to move the stove during the task.

Sometimes it is actually helpful to have the sun move. You may want to cook something and then keep it simmering a long time, or just keep it warm for later eating. Just leave the stove in one position for this kind of adjustable temperature; the sun does the rest by moving. Because of this, your solar hot plate has a built-in automatic timer! Try this technique: when you finish cooking lunch, leave the hot plate set up at that angle. Next day put on the food anytime during the morning and then go on about your business. At the proper time, the sun moves into the right position, the hot plate heats up, and dinner is cooking! Some campers do this with the morning coffee: they leave the hot plate pointing at the early morning sun, prepare the percolator, and go to bed. Next morning they awake to the sounds, sights, and smells of fresh coffee brewing.

The solar hot plate has limitations, of course. Since it is a concentrating mirror, it uses only the *direct* rays of the sun. It works best on a bright clear day when the sky is deep blue; take it along next time you go to the mountains and you will notice a big difference in clear, thin mountain air. On a cloudy or hazy day, there is less direct radiation and your solar stove will not perform as well.

The amount of radiation which reaches the solar cooker is in direct proportion to the position of the sun. When the sun is low its rays reach you through a thicker layer of smoke, dust, and other pollution that screens the direct rays. So you will cook hotter and faster at noon than you will at 9 AM or 5 PM. You can cook at those hours too if you allow a bit more time to get the job done. But because the reflector will be almost upright, be sure you don't put too much weight on the grill and tip everything over! When using the stove in early morning or late in the day, you may have to add some weight to the top of the reflector. We use a piece of wood 2" x 4" x 30".

A length of 2" x 4" board, placed on top of the box, keeps a pot of beans from upsetting the reflector.

TIPS FOR YOUR SOLAR HOT PLATE

We quickly learned that flat black paint makes the best grill, pot, or pan better. Spray paint the *outside* surfaces of your solar cooking utensils and they will work faster. Put them on the grill in bright sunshine before using them. The paint will smoke and get nicely baked on. This way you also won't get a paint taste in your food.

Use pots and pans large enough to accept all the solar energy your stove reflects onto the grill. A big pot is generally better than one that is small. For hot cakes, or for searing a steak or hamburger we find that a skillet with a thick bottom works well. It stores up a lot of heat that is transferred to the food when you put it in the pan. For something that will take a lot of cooking, be sure to cover the pot to keep the heat in. Because the solar hot plate is not as sturdy as the kitchen range, we use aluminum utensils in most cases, although a small steel pot or pan is not too heavy.

We have found that a slight accumulation of dust (and even grease, etc.) doesn't greatly reduce the cooking power of the solar hot plate. But clean the reflector once in a while. A "tack cloth" available from a paint store is handy for removing dust quickly. Grease can be removed with warm water and detergent. The aluminized mylar is very durable because of its tough plastic coating. If you have used aluminum foil, use care in cleaning and handling so it will last a long time.

One word of warning: Don't let your solar hot plate get wet! Water and cardboard don't mix well, so keep the cooker out of rainy or damp weather.

A black solar coffee pot perks faster!

4
OTHER COOKERS

We think our two solar cookers are great, and we hope you will build them. The tips we have given, and the many recipes we have tested, can also be used with other solar cookers. We have used a number of them and found several that work well. Some are quite compact and suitable for camping trips where cooking needs are not so great.

Our favorite commercial solar hot plate unfortunately is no longer available. We bought our Umbroiler about 20 years ago and it still works well even though it is a bit frayed around the edges. The invention of Dr. George Löf, a leading solar scientist, it is named for the umbrella it is made from.

The beauty of the Umbroiler is that it folds up just like an umbrella. And as someone said, even if it rains you can still use it to keep dry. Easy to carry in the trunk of a car, or even slung over your back, the Umbroiler generates lots of heat and will make coffee, cook hamburgers, hot dogs and steak. It heats water to do the dishes, too.

Our 20-year-old Umbroiler still works very well.

The best commercial solar oven we've used has to be Sam Erwin's Solar Chef. Using real mirrors, it produces high temperatures and will cook just about anything. For fun, Sam built a monster Super Chef twice the size of the standard model. We watched it cook 40 pounds of beef in Phoenix one afternoon for a big solar dinner. We have fitted our Solar Chef with a table top, so that after it has cooked a solar meal we can eat right on top of it. A real conversation piece for back yard or patio, it is quite large and heavy and not the kind of cooker you travel with.

In the back of this book you will find a listing of some of the marketers of solar cooking equipment. They also sell such things as solar showers, simple black rubber bags that heat enough water for a quick bath. You may also want a solar water heater, or even a solar still. If you want to build your own we suggest you get a copy of our earlier book, *Solar Science Projects*, as it has plans and instruction for these and several other fun projects.

The sun can power many different devices. You can have a solar radio, light your cigarettes with a solar lighter, or even buy a solar-powered calculator! But we still think that solar cookery is the most pleasant and impressive demonstration of sun power. Give it a try!

The Solar Chef oven in constructed of real mirrors.

4
INTRODUCTION
TO SOLAR COOKING

Twenty years ago when I started cooking with a solar oven and reflector cooker, it was a novelty — a lark. We liked to have friends, Boy Scouts, and others interested in solar energy over to see how we could cook with the sun. Occasionally we enjoyed taking these cookers along on a picnic or outing. Today I cook with sunshine for a different reason.

Since the energy crunch, my outlook has changed from a once-in-a-while demonstration of a novel method of cooking to a way of life. Many friends have told me that they are excited about cooking outdoors, especially in the summer when they don't want to heat up the house. Some people cut down on baking in the summer months because of the expense of air conditioning. Solar cookery makes it possible to bake without heating up the house.

The recipe section is the result of my experiences over the past twenty years with solar cookery. Many people have helped with recipes that I've adapted for the solar oven and reflector cooker. These recipes, varied as they are, will be just an introduction to solar cooking. I really believe that just about any dish can be cooked with solar energy.

Start with simple recipes so that you avoid problems. Many things are very easy to cook with the solar oven and reflector cooker, so don't start with a complicated cake or gourmet meat dish first time out. After a little practice, don't hesitate to try your own favorites and to experiment with solar cookery in your own way. Let us know your successes — and failures, too! Maybe we can include them when it's time to do another edition of *Solar Cookery*.

Carefully read the following solar cooking tips before attempting to cook a meal on your new solar cookers. These helpful tips will familiarize you with the differences between conventional and solar cooking.

Sun

Locate the most constantly sunny place in your yard. When I get up in the morning, I think not only of meal-planning but also about what kind of solar day it is. If it's exceptionally clear and sunny, I might decide to do some extra baking — like a special cake. I automatically go out in the morning and set up my oven and focus it so that it is hot and "ready to go" when I decide to bake bread, put together a casserole, or simply defrost something. I constantly *think solar*.

Cookware

You can use any kind of cookware, but dark, lightweight cookware heats up faster. Shiny steel or aluminum pans reflect away some of the heat, making them less efficient. I do use my aluminum pans, but the older the better, and you should consider spray-painting the exterior black for more heat absorption. However, one of my favorite casserole dishes is a heavy pottery dish. It takes longer to heat up, but once hot, holds the heat better.

Don't use aluminum foil around your meat or vegetables, or as a cover for a casserole. The aluminum foil will reflect the heat too. Use a Reynolds oven bag.

Focus

Perhaps the biggest difference between your kitchen oven and your solar oven is that the heating element of the one in the kitchen stays still, while the sun, which heats your solar oven, is always moving. It moves slowly, but we do have to remember that eventually we must move the oven or reflector cooker to keep the heat where we want it.

The morning sun is very low in the sky, so we must aim our cookers quite low to catch its rays. The same thing is true in late afternoon, and shortly before sunset we are done with solar cooking because the sun is too low.

Don't worry about aiming the solar oven and reflector stove. It's done with shadows and is very easy. In a few days you will be an expert on how fast (or how slow) the sun moves, and how to adjust the oven for best results and desired temperatures. Remember that when there is no shadow from the nail in the knob, the oven is pointing directly at the sun.

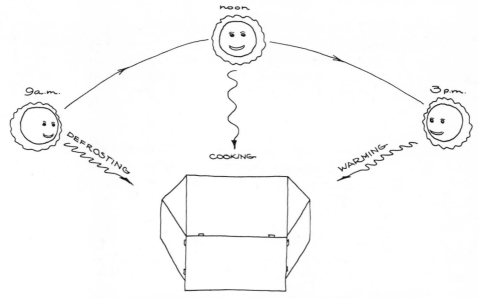

USING "AUTOMATIC TIMING" WITH THE SOLAR OVEN

You will find that you can make use of the automatic timer offered by the sun's movement. With experience you will be able to aim the cooker to a point where the sun will be in a few hours. This will let you put food in the oven early, have it cook, and then keep warm for some time. You can even use this technique to defrost and then cook with one setting. See the drawing for a clearer picture of this method.

Temperatures and Cooking Times

Most of the recipes are geared to cook at approximately 300° unless otherwise designated. This is because there is little difficulty in getting the oven up to 350°. When the food is placed in the oven, the density and temperature of the food will cause the oven temperature to drop. However, most food, except the desserts, can be cooked at lower temperatures. Just leave the food in the oven longer. You will find more specific instructions on timing at the beginning of each chapter.

Solar cooking is not the same as setting a thermostat and timing with a clock. At first you must watch more carefully and see exactly how long something is going to take. For meats, the timing is about the same as inside. You can be sure by investing in an inexpensive meat thermometer. However, for bread, cookies, and cakes, you will not always have as high a solar oven temperature as in your gas or electric oven. Adjust the timing accordingly and you will find that you can cook just about anything. You really can bake cakes at a lower temperature than in the house. It just takes longer.

Pre-heating the Oven

It is usually advisable to pre-heat your solar oven before starting to cook, unless you are using your oven to defrost something first. It will take thirty to forty minutes for the oven to warm up, depending on sky conditions.

Sunglasses

The solar cookers reflect a lot of heat, and also a great deal of light. I always wear sunglasses when cooking because of the light intensity. The glasses protect your eyes and make it easier to see inside the oven. The reflection from the solar hot plate can be even stronger.

Oven Racks

We have devised a swinging rack to keep the food level when the oven is tilted for focus. We recommend an inexpensive cooling rack to be used when the oven is flat. As good cooks know, this allows heat to circulate under the food and cook it evenly.

Seasons

Remember that in the winter the sun rises later and sets sooner. Also that it is very low in the sky even at noon. All you do is aim your solar cooker at the sun and it will do its job. Wintertime direction is a constant low-in-the-sky focus.

You will find that you have several more hours a day during the summer months (May through September). Because the sun is higher in the sky, you will have a hotter oven. It is during these months that you will most enjoy cooking the high-temperature recipes.

A pot of tea is brewing on the solar hot plate at an altitude of 7000 feet and a temperature of 32° F. Note the shadow of pot at center of the reflector.

Geography of Solar Cooking

If you have a sunny spot in your yard, it doesn't matter whether you live in Arizona or Maine. There can be snow on the ground as long as there is sunshine. The temperature of the cookers is determined by the amount of sunshine, not by the outside temperature.

Recently some relatives from Utah were visiting and their reactions to my solar bread-baking were interesting. They said, "Sure, it works here in Phoenix where it's hot, but it wouldn't work in Utah." They were so wrong! It could work better in Utah where the air is clear in the higher altitude.

Weather

Let's face it, there are times when the sun just doesn't cooperate. So don't get rid of your inside cooking equipment. Consider it a "backup" to your solar cookers and use it when you have to. At the same time, don't always let cloudy weather chase you indoors. Clouds move and the sky may clear again, so try to work with the weather.

The solar oven is a combination reflector and flat plate cooker. The flat plate part, the glass door, works well even under an overcast sky. I've cooked roast and vegetables on slightly overcast days, when I wondered if it was going to work, and was amazed at the performance of the oven. The reflector stove, on the other hand, must have a clear sky because it is like a big lens and won't work without the direct rays of the sun.

Solar cooks, aged 8 and 9, frying eggs for breakfast.

Solar Hot Plate Cooking

Most of what I have said applies to our solar oven. This is because for me it is the workhorse of the cooking team. For steaks, hamburgers, and hot dogs, plus breakfasts of bacon and eggs and hotcakes, the solar hot plate can't be beat. You won't believe it the first time you see, hear, and smell coffee perking on your reflector stove.

I use the reflector for cooking sauces and gravies, soups, lentils, beans, and other vegetables. And, of course, for heating water for various purposes.

Whenever the recipes say to simmer, turn the reflector cooker slightly off focus so the grill won't be too hot.

Don't overload the grill. I use a lightweight 1-1/2 quart pan for cooking the sauces, soups, beans, etc., and an 8" frying pan for bacon, eggs, steak, and hamburger. These, along with our 6 cup coffee pot have been spray-painted black for maximum heat absorption.

As described in Chapter 3, it is possible to weight the cooker down in the back to prevent tipping. Handled with care your cooker will perform well and last a long time.

SYMBOLS

The recipes which are keyed for high sun cook the fastest and best on clear sunny days. The cakes and pies should always be cooked as close to noon as possible. The low sun recipes do well in the morning, late afternoon, and in the winter. Some recipes can be cooked with either kind of conditions but they take much longer with low sun, or they might cook faster than you would wish with high sun. Recipes which have not been keyed for either type of sun position can be cooked easily with either high or low sun.

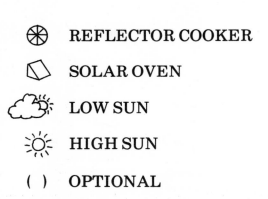

⊛   REFLECTOR COOKER

◇   SOLAR OVEN

☁☀   LOW SUN

☀   HIGH SUN

( )   OPTIONAL

6
BREADS

It might surprise you to know that the solar oven lends itself very well to baking bread. One of the questions most frequently asked is, "Does the bread brown, and are the rolls light?" The answer is "yes" to both questions. Just be willing to take as long as is needed to get the bread as brown as you want it. One day I baked four dozen rolls for two hours. It was an overcast day and the sun kept popping in and out from behind the clouds, causing the temperature to vary quite radically. But the rolls were light, brown, and delicious.

It has been said that many people have never tasted real bread. This refers to those who have only eaten "store-bought" bread and have never experienced the enjoyment that comes from eating a loaf of home-baked bread. I like to consider nutrition when baking breads, so I use unbleached white flour as well as the other natural grains. Also, I substitute natural sugar, or honey, or molasses for the processed sugar that is often used in recipes.

In considering the amount of flour used in these recipes, remember that it is almost impossible to give an exact amount for each recipe because of the difference in the characteristics of flour, as well as variations in the atmosphere. Therefore, when a recipe calls for kneading in extra flour, just knead in as much as you need to achieve a dough that is not sticky and has a good consistency.

As with cakes, the middle of the day is best for solar bread-making. The recipes in this chapter are planned for about a 300° - 325° oven. If the air is very clear and the oven reaches a higher temperature, all the better.

First, let your oven reach its maximum temperature. If 350° is your maximum, the temperature will probably drop to around 300° or 325° after you put in the bread, muffins, or rolls. Then it may rise again slowly. Learn what your variables are, be a little adventuresome, and you'll become as addicted to baking bread in your solar oven as I am. It's fun!

Your oven can also be used in wintertime as a place to let the dough rise. Simply turn the oven so that it is off focus and doesn't warm too much.

TIPS FOR BREAD RECIPES

1. If the recipe calls for sour milk, you can make sweet milk sour by adding 1-1/2 tablespoons of lemon juice or 1-1/3 tablespoons of vinegar to each cup of milk.
2. If you want a soft crust, simply brush the bread with butter while it is still warm.
3. When the recipe is for two loaves and you want to bake one loaf at a time, simply keep the second loaf in the refrigerator after it has risen the second time. Then let it return to room temperature and bake.
4. Keep dough out of a draft while it is rising.
5. Sourdough starter is usually obtainable at any gourmet shop. However, you can make your own. All you need is flour, sugar, water, and patience. To get your starter started, just put some flour, sugar, and lukewarm water together and let it sit on the back of your stove or somewhere else where it will remain at a fairly warm, constant temperature. It should *not* cook. A temperature of 80° - 90° F is about right.

    Eventually the yeast spores in the air will get into the mixture and start growing, thus beginning the process of fermentation. You can tell when it has begun by the bubbling of the mix and by the typical yeast odor. The yeast organisms will, of course, be growing all the time in the mixture, so that after a while you have a bowlful of active yeast. Refrigerate the starter to keep it fresh.

    To keep the starter alive you must use a little every week. To replenish the sourdough starter add 1/2 cup of flour mixed with 1/2 cup condensed milk.
6. Remember that you can cook bread and rolls at lower temperatures if you just adjust the cooking time accordingly.

TEXAS BISCUITS

I will never be able to make biscuits like my mother did. There was just something about her touch. She told me that on the ranch when her brothers were out on a round-up, they just made the biscuits in the top of the flour sack, not even using a bowl. She said to use two walnut size dabs of shortening for this recipe. As near as I can figure out, that would be about two tablespoons. Here is her recipe.

2 cups flour
3 rounded tsp. baking powder
1 tsp. salt
1 tbsp. sugar
1 cup milk
2 tbsp. shortening

Combine dry ingredients and cut in shortening. Make a hole in the middle of the dry ingredients and add milk. Work into a ball and knead lightly, then roll out and with a cutter dipped in flour, cut your biscuits. Dip each side of your biscuit in melted butter or oil and place on your sheet pan. You can stack another biscuit on top and press ever so lightly together, or leave them single. Bake at 325° for about 40 minutes. Makes 2 dozen medium biscuits.

SOURDOUGH BLUEBERRY MUFFINS

½ cup whole wheat flour
1½ cups white flour
½ cup vegetable oil
½ cup sugar
½ cup evaporated milk
1 egg
¾ tsp. baking soda
½ tsp. salt
1 cup fresh or frozen blueberries, raisins, or lingonberries
¾ cup sourdough starter

Mix together the first eight ingredients *in order of their listing*, adding enough sourdough starter to make the mixture moist and hold together nicely. *Do not* beat vigorously. Fold in the frozen blueberries very gently, to avoid turning your dough purple. Drop in greased muffin tins; the cups should be half full. Bake for 40 minutes at 325°. Nice light-medium brown when done. Makes 18 medium muffins.

CEREAL MUFFINS

It's always fun to discover a good recipe when dining with friends, and then find that it works well in the solar oven. This is a favorite.

1 cup all bran cereal
1 cup crushed shredded wheat
1 cup boiling water
½ cup shortening
1½ cups sugar or 1 cup honey
2 eggs
2 cups buttermilk
1 cup quick oatmeal
2½ cups flour
2½ tsp. baking soda
1½ tsp. salt

Combine bran cereal and crushed shredded wheat; cover with boiling water. *Do not* stir. Cool to lukewarm. Cream shortening, sugar or honey, and eggs. Add buttermilk and oatmeal to creamed ingredients. Sift flour, soda, and salt together; add to egg and shortening mixture. Add the cooled cereals, stirring briefly. Bake in muffin tins at 325° for 45-55 minutes. Makes one dozen muffins.

EASY BANANA SANDWICH BREAD

½ cup butter
1 cup sugar
2 eggs
3 crushed bananas
½ cup butter
1 tsp. baking soda
Pinch of salt
¼ cup broken pecan meats

Cream butter and sugar; beat in eggs. Add bananas and beat well. Mix in flour, soda, and salt. Stir in nuts. Pour into greased 9" x 5" x 3" pan and bake 1 hour at 300°-325°. Makes one loaf.

MEXICAN SPOON BREAD

This is a moist spoon bread that is served with a tomato sauce over the top. With a tossed salad and a vegetable it can be a main course.

Bread

> 1 lb. can cream style corn or 3 ears of fresh, uncooked corn
> 1 cup corn meal
> ⅓ cup melted shortening
> 2 eggs
> 1 tsp. salt
> ⅓ tsp. baking soda
> ⅔ of a 4 oz. can green chilis, drained and chopped
>   (reserve ⅓ of the can for the sauce)
> 1 ½ cups shredded cheddar cheese

Combine the first five ingredients and mix well. When using the fresh corn, simply scrape the kernels from the corn cobs and combine with the remaining ingredients. Pour half of the batter into a greased 8" square pan. Sprinkle with green chilis and half of the cheese. Pour the remaining batter on top and sprinkle with the other half of the cheese; bake for about 1-1/3 hours at 300°-325°.

Sauce

> 1 lb. can of stewed tomatoes
> 8 oz. can tomato sauce
> reserved chopped green chilis
> 1 tsp. salt
> pepper
> ¼ tsp. oregano

Chop the tomatoes until they are chunky. Combine with the remaining ingredients and simmer on the reflector for about 1/2 hour. Pour the sauce over the baked bread. Makes 6 - 8 servings.

OLD-FASHIONED CORNBREAD

2 cups corn meal
2 cups sour milk or buttermilk
1 tsp. baking soda
1 tbsp. sugar
2 tbsp. shortening, melted
1 tsp. salt
1 egg

Mix dry ingredients. Add milk, beaten egg, and shortening. Pour into 8" square pan and bake for 40 minutes at 300°. Makes one 8" square bread.

LIGHT ROLLS

One of the breads that makes the biggest hit with our family is just a plain light roll. Remember that dough for rolls is softer than for plain bread, as soft as can be handled without sticking to hands or board. Once I learned that rolls require only thorough mixing, with little or no kneading, I began to have a lot more success with roll-making.

1 cup milk, scalded
2 tbsp. shortening
2 tbsp. sugar
1 tsp. salt
1 cake fresh or 1 package dry yeast
¼ cup lukewarm water
1 egg
3 cups flour

Combine milk, shortening, sugar, and salt; cool to lukewarm. Add yeast softened in lukewarm water. Beat the egg well and add to mixed ingredients. Beat vigorously; cover and let rise in warm place (80° - 90°) until doubled in bulk, about 2 hours. Turn out on lightly floured surface and shape into your preferred shape for rolls. I like to shape 2" size balls, flatten and roll, and place in the pan. Let rise until double in size again. Then bake at 300° - 325° until nice and brown on top. Makes 2 dozen rolls.

HELEN'S WHEAT BREAD

1 package dry yeast
½ tsp. sugar
¼ cup lukewarm water
1 cup lukewarm water with 4 tbsp. melted margarine or butter
1 egg, beaten
1 tbsp. salt
¼ cup sugar or 2 tbsp. honey
1½ cups white flour
2 cups wheat flour

Mix yeast, 1/2 tsp. sugar, and 1/4 cup water; let stand 10 minutes. Combine water and butter, egg, salt, sugar or honey; add to yeast mixture. Add 1-1/2 cups white flour and beat well. Slowly add wheat flour, beating well. Knead the bread until it is smooth (about 10 minutes). Place in a large, well-oiled bowl and turn the dough so that it is oiled on all sides. Let rise until double in bulk (about 1 1/2 hours). Punch down and form into 2 loaves and put into oiled bread pans to rise until double in size again. Bake at 325° for about 55 minutes. The bread is done when it sounds hollow when tapped on the top. Makes one large loaf.

CORNELL BREAD

The woman who gave me this recipe said that it is so nutritious that she can have a couple pieces of toast from this bread in the morning with a glass of orange juice, play eighteen holes of golf, and have energy to spare.

3 packages of dry yeast
3 cups warm water
⅓ cup molasses
1⅔ tbsp. vegetable oil
5 cups whole wheat flour, sifted
5 tbsp. soy flour
7½ oz. non-fat dry milk
4 tbsp. wheat germ
2½ tbsp. brewer's yeast
2 tbsp. salt

Mix yeast, water, and molasses; let stand 5 minutes. Add 1-2/3 tbsp. oil to yeast mixture. Combine remaining ingredients and stir into yeast mixture. It will be a sticky dough. Turn onto a floured board and knead until smooth, adding flour as needed. Turn into greased bread tins and let rise. It is a heavy dough, so will not double in size. Bake at 325° - 350° for 1 hour and 15 minutes. Makes 2 loaves.

FRENCH-ITALIAN BREAD

This is probably the most simple white bread recipe ever devised. It also happens to be our favorite, and we never tire of it.

1 package active dry yeast
1 cup warm water (110° F)
1½ tsp. sugar
1 tsp. salt
2 - 3 cups flour
¼ cup corn meal

Dissolve the yeast in water in large bowl. Add sugar, salt, and 1 cup of flour. Beat until thoroughly blended. Gradually stir in the remaining flour until the batter is quite stiff. Then knead in any flour necessary to make a nice smooth dough. Knead for ten minutes and then turn into a well-oiled bowl, turning so that the dough is oiled all over. Cover and let rise for 90 minutes or until double in size. Punch down, remove from bowl, and let stand on floured board for 10 mintues. Form into a long loaf. Place on a greased cookie sheet dusted with corn meal. Slash top of loaf diagonally. (You can also form a regular loaf and place it in an oiled bread pan.) Let rise 90 minutes. Bake for about 45 minutes to 1 hour at 325°. Brush top of crust with melted margarine or salt water solution, depending on taste. Makes one loaf.

LIMPA

This is a Swedish rye bread. A novel bread pan that makes an unusual round loaf is a clay flower pot dish (the part you set the pot in), lined with foil and oiled. The bread comes out round, and it tastes delicious because of the properties of the clay dish.

2 cups milk (sweet or sour)
⅔ cup dark molasses
¼ cup melted shortening
1 package dry yeast
¼ cup lukewarm water
2 cups unbleached white flour
2 tsp. salt
2 cups rye flour
2 cups whole wheat flour
(3 tbsp. caraway seed or grated peel of 1 large orange)

Sift flours, then measure separately. Dissolve the yeast in 1/4 cup luke-warm water and let stand for 10 minutes. Add the yeast, salt, and molasses to the milk. Add the caraway seed or orange peel, if you are using either. Slowly beat in 1-3/4 cups of white flour. Add the shortening. Gradually stir in the rye and whole wheat flours to make a stiff dough. Sprinkle the remaining 1/4 cup of flour on a breadboard and turn out the stiff dough onto the board; cover with the bowl and let stand for 10 minutes. Then knead lightly for 10 minutes. Round into a ball and return to washed, greased bowl, turning once to bring greased side up. Cover and let rise in a warm place until double, about 1-1/2 hours. Turn dough onto lightly floured board, cut in half, round up portions, cover with bowls, and let stand 10 minutes. Shape into loaves and place in bread pans and let double in size again (about 1-1/2 hours). Bake for 1 - 1/2 hours, with middle-of-the-day sun. Cook one loaf at a time. When done turn out of the pan at once to cool. Makes 2 round loaves.

CROWN COFFEECAKE

5 cups flour
2 packages dry yeast
¼ cup warm water
¾ cup milk
½ cup sugar
2 tsp. salt
¾ cup butter, melted
2 eggs, beaten
½ cup slivered almonds
2 tsp. cinnamon

Dissolve yeast in warm water. Beat together 1-1/2 cups flour, yeast and water, warm milk, 1/2 cup sugar, salt, and margarine. Add beaten eggs and another cup of flour. Beat until the batter is smooth. Slowly add the rest of the flour until you have a light, smooth dough. Place in buttered bowl and brush with 1/2 cup melted butter. Cover, put in a warm place, and let rise until double in size. (This dough is very slow-rising.) Punch down and let stand 10 minutes. Combine cinnamon and 1 cup sugar. Sprinkle the bottom of a 10" tube pan with the almonds and 1-1/2 tbsp. of the sugar-cinnamon mixture. Pinch off pieces of dough and shape in balls 1-1/2" in diameter. Roll in the remaining 1/4 cup melted butter and then in the sugar mix. Place in the tube pan and let rise until double in size. Bake in a 325° oven for about an hour. Makes one large loaf.

SOURDOUGH PANCAKES

Sourdough pancakes are great made on the reflector cooker, and any leftover dough can be turned into a dough for light rolls.

½ cup sourdough starter
1 cup undiluted evaporated milk
1 cup warm water
1¾ - 2 cups flour
2 eggs
2 tbsp. sugar
½ tsp. salt
1 tsp. baking soda

Combine starter, milk, water, and flour in a large bowl: mix to blend and leave at room temperature overnight. Next morning add eggs, sugar, salt, and baking soda; mix well. *Don't beat.* Cook on a greased griddle over medium heat. Turn when the top side is full of broken bubbles and has lost its glossiness. Makes 30 3'' pancakes.

SOURDOUGH HOT ROLLS

Leftover pancake batter can be used for sourdough rolls. Simply add flour and salt. The proportion of flour to salt is 1 cup flour to 1/2 tsp. salt. The amount you need will depend on how much batter you have left. Just keep adding the flour mixture until the consistency is right.

1 recipe of Sourdough Pancakes
2 cups flour
1 tsp. salt

Mix ingredients and turn out on a floured board. Knead, adding flour as necessary, until it is a smooth ball. Place in a greased bowl, brush with melted butter and let rise for about 1 hour. Punch down and knead again, adding flour if needed. Roll out to about 3/4'' thick. Cut with cutter, dip each roll on both sides in melted butter, and place just touching in the pan. Cover, let rise until doubled (about 1 hour). Bake at 325° for 45 minutes. Makes 2 dozen rolls.

PIZZA

For best results plan to cook your pizza at noon when the oven is level and the sun directly overhead.

Dough

½ cup warm water
4 tsp. vegetable oil
½ tsp. salt
1 package dry yeast
1½ cups flour

Combine water, 1 tsp. vegetable oil, salt, and dry yeast. *Don't stir.* Let stand 5 minutes. Knead in flour and then 3 tsp. of vegetable oil.

Sauce

1 8 oz. can tomato sauce
1 clove garlic, minced
½ medium onion, grated
½ tsp. Italian seasoning
¼ tsp. salt
¾ cup shredded mozzarella cheese

Combine the ingredients, except the cheese, in a saucepan and simmer on the reflector cooker for 10 minutes or until slightly thick. Spread the dough in a 13" round pan. Spread sauce on top and sprinkle with cheese. Bake at 325° for 1/2 hour. Makes one 13" pizza. Other cheeses (cheddar or provolone), green peppers, mushrooms, or pepperoni can be added after cheese.

7
VEGETABLES

According to nutritionist Adele Davis in *Let's Cook It Right*, whenever vegetables are cooked with water, the vitamins are leached out and lost. Baking is far superior to boiling as a method of cooking vegetables. The solar oven lends itself beautifully to this nutritious and tasty way of preparing vegetables, legumes, and vegetable casserole dishes. The reflector cooker is used to saute, boil, or steam.

When baking in the solar oven, remember to warm up the oven first. Wash the vegetables and put them in a plastic oven bag, close with a twistee, and place in the oven. For additional nutrition and flavor you can place the vegetables, plastic bag and all, in a brown grocery bag before inserting in the oven. You can cook them in a covered casserole dish. The vegetables should cook as quickly as possible in the beginning. After they are warmed through, slow cooking is best so that they do not shrivel and become unattractive and tasteless. I wash my oven bags and reuse them as an economy measure. Do *not* use ordinary plastic bags for cooking — they aren't designed for that and could have toxins in them.

Do *not* add water or salt to the vegetables. You can add other spices for flavor, but salt will draw the vitamins from the vegetables, so try to add the salt right before serving if it's at all possible. Cooking the vegetables whole takes longer, but the vitamins are more apt to escape from cut vegetables. However, when the vegetable is cut, trimmed, or grated, add a little vegetable or olive oil to coat it and seal in the juices. This will prevent unnecessary loss of vitamin C. Do *not* use butter or margarine until just before serving; if cooked with the vegetables, the butter or margarine lose valuable vitamin A.

If you eat a lot of vegetables, as we do, much of the time you will simply wash and clean the vegetables and cook them plain. We find that the vegetables have so much more flavor when cooked in the solar oven that we enjoy them this way.

One thing I like to do is combine two or more vegetables, then add some onion slices, a clove of garlic, bell pepper pieces if I have one on hand, and even chunks of fresh tomato — or any combination of these. We like to use a little olive oil with our vegetables; if used sparingly there isn't a strong taste of olive oil and yet there is a nice flavor and additional nutrition. I sometimes put several kinds of squash together. If I want to give the dish an Italian flavor, I add a little basil or a combination of the Italian seasonings.

Sometimes I grate a good cheese (one that has been aged at least six months), empty the vegetables into a serving dish, sprinkle with the cheese, and place it back in the oven for a few minutes to allow the cheese to melt over the vegetables. My family really loves the vegetables this way. For added nutrition and flavor, you can sprinkle with sesame or hulled sunflower seeds.

Because the vegetables are often somewhat cold when placed in a 350° oven, the temperature will drop to 325° or lower. It will take about 45 minutes for vegetables like squash or cauliflower pieces to cook. If the vegetables are grated, cooking time is greatly reduced.

MAYONNAISE AND YOGURT SAUCE

I like to serve this as a vegetable topping.

1 cup mayonnaise
1 cup yogurt
2 tbsp. lemon juice or vinegar
1 tsp. salt
1 tsp. Worcestershire Sauce
½ tsp. dry mustard
2 - 4 tbsp. grated onion
2 tbsp. finely chopped parsley
Dash cayenne

Combine ingredients in order listed. Blend well. Makes 2 cups.

SHREDDED BEETS

Grated beets will be eaten by people who would ordinarily spurn this vegetable.

4 - 6 medium beets
1 tbsp. lemon juice or 2 tbsp. vegetable oil
½ tsp. salt
1 tbsp. butter or margaine

Wash beets thoroughly. Trim and shred, but *do not* peel. Toss with either the lemon juice or oil. Cook in the oven for 1/2 hour. Add salt and butter or margarine. Serve piping hot, but crisp. Serves 4.

GRATED CARROTS

6 carrots
8 oz. can crushed pineapple, well-drained
½ cup raisins
Nutmeg
Salt

Grate the carrots coarsely. Place in an oven bag or covered heated casserole dish with the pineapple and raisins; cook in a 300° - 325° oven for about 20 - 30 minutes. Season with salt and a little nutmeg when removed from the oven. Serves 4.

SAUTÉED ZUCCHINI

3 medium zucchinis, sliced
¼ cup oil
juice of 1 lemon
1 garlic clove
Salt

Saute the squash in the hot oil, lemon juice, and garlic. Cook until nice and crisp. Some of the chips might be a little transparent, but serve this squash very crisp. Salt to taste before serving. Serves 4.

DILLED ZUCCHINI

2 medium zucchini
½ tsp. dill weed
1 tbsp. melted butter

Cut 2 unpared medium zucchini lengthwise in half. Place in an oven bag and cook until tender, about 40 minutes. Brush with melted butter and sprinkle with dill weed. Makes 4 servings.

BAKED ZUCCHINI

2 zucchini
1 tbsp. butter
Salt
Pepper

Wash and slice in round chips and cook in a plastic bag in your solar oven for at least 30 minutes for a semi-soft squash. Season with salt, pepper, and butter. Serves 4.

BUTTERNUT SQUASH

1 butternut squash
¼ cup butter
½ cup brown sugar

Cut the squash in half and clean the fibrous insides and seeds from the squash. Place with the cut side down on a flat pan and cook in the solar oven for an hour or more at 275°. Then turn the squash over and sprinkle with the sugar and dot with the butter. Return to oven and cook for another 15 minutes. Serves 2 - 4.

GREEN BEANS

2 lbs. green beans

Wash and string the beans. Cut the way you prefer, break into sections, or leave whole. Place in an oven bag and cook at 300° or better for at least an hour. The length of time depends on how crisp you like your vegetables. Serves 6 - 8.

POTATOES

My preference is to cook red potatoes in a plastic oven bag. If you prefer Irish potatoes, do get your oven as hot as possible. It helps them to cook more quickly if you insert a nail in each one. The more potatoes you cook, the more they will reduce the heat of the oven. Potatoes pull the heat down more than meat will, so if you are having a crowd for dinner, consider settling for the smaller red potatoes that don't need as hot an oven.

ITALIAN FRIED LETTUCE

Use the outer leaves of iceberg lettuce (the ones you usually throw away) or romaine lettuce.

6 - 8 lettuce leaves
2 tbsp. olive or vegetable oil
1 clove garlic, minced
Salt
(2 slices beef bacon)
(leftover cooked vegetables)

If using the bacon, cut it into small pieces and brown well. Chop your leftover vegetables and brown them in the oil and garlic. Add the lettuce leaves and cook quickly, stirring constantly; the lettuce is done when it is transparent. Season with salt. Serves 4.

CORN

Husk, wash and trim fresh corn. Leave it on the cob and place in an oven bag. Cook for 20 minutes at 300° - 350°. It tastes just like steamed corn!

CORN PUDDING

8 - 10 medium ears of corn or 3 cups canned corn
1 tsp. sugar
2 tbsp. flour
3 eggs
1 tsp. salt
⅓ tsp. pepper
3 tsp. butter
Dash cayenne
Dash nutmeg

Scrape corn over large shredding surface of a food grater, letting pulp fall into a large bowl; also scrape each cob with back of a knife to remove all pulp. If using canned corn make sure it is well-drained. Combine with sugar, flour, eggs, salt, pepper, cayenne, and nutmeg, stirring with a fork to blend well. Pour into an ungreased shallow 1 qt. casserole. Dot corn with butter. Bake, uncovered, in a 300° oven for 1 hour, or until pudding is set in the center when gently shaken. Spoon out to serve. Serves 4 - 6.

COLE SLAW

This is so easy to make, and yet so well-received.

¾ cup vinegar
½ cup sugar
1½ tsp. salt
1 tsp. dry mustard
1 cup salad oil
1 medium head of cabbage
2-3 green onions
(1 carrot, shredded)
(4 leaves red lettuce)

Combine first four ingredients in saucepan and bring to boil. Remove from heat and add 1 cup salad oil. Shred cabbage and green onions. If desired add a little shredded carrot and red lettuce for color. Pour liquid over the cabbage, onions, and carrot mixture. Cover tightly. Refrigerate overnight. Serves 8 - 10.

BROCCOLI AND RICE

This is a good way to use the stems of your broccoli which you might otherwise discard. Be sure to peel them (the tough outer skin can be taken off very easily). Then cook them in a covered pan with a little water on top of the reflector cooker. Then chop and combine with any leftover tops you might have.

1½ cups of chopped broccoli, cooked
2 cups cooked rice
1 cup sour cream
10¾ oz. can cream of chicken soup
Salt
Pepper

Combine broccoli, rice, sour cream, undiluted chicken soup, salt, and pepper and place in an oiled casserole. Bake for 45 minutes to an hour until firm. Serves 4.

ARTICHOKE AND LIMA BEAN SUPREME

This is the most delightful vegetable combination I have ever tasted. It is a little more expensive than the usual vegetable dish, but worth the price for a special occasion. It is so good that it can even be served cold, once cooked. The friend with whom this recipe originated likes to use fresh vegetables, but since they are hard to obtain in some areas, this recipe will include frozen vegetables. If you're cooking for a crowd, other vegetables can be added, such as tiny baby peas and asparagus.

1 9 oz. package frozen baby artichokes
1 10 oz. package frozen baby lima beans
1 tbsp. olive oil
1 clove garlic, minced
1 tsp. salt
Bac-O-Bits

Combine the partially thawed vegetables in an oven bag. Add the oil and garlic and place in the solar oven at 300°. Heat until hot. Season with the salt and after pouring into the serving dish, sprinkle with Bac-O-Bits. Serves 6.

STRING BEANS SUPREME

1 10 oz. package frozen string beans or 1 lb. fresh beans
½ cup chopped onion
1 cup sour cream
4 tbsp. margarine or butter
1 cup bread crumbs
½ cup grated cheddar cheese

If you are using fresh beans cook them in a small amount of water on the reflector cooker. Saute the chopped onion in 2 tbsp. of butter, add string beans and mix together with the sour cream. Brown the bread crumbs in 2 tbsp. melted margarine or butter, sprinkle over the string bean mixture, and top with the grated cheese. Bake in the solar oven until the cheese is melted and the other ingredients are hot, about 30 - 45 minutes. Serves 4 - 6.

AVOCADO SOUP

3 cups chicken or vegetable broth
¼ cup chopped onions
2 tbsp. vegetable oil
2 small zucchini, thinly sliced
1 tsp. seasoning salt
¼ cup lemon juice
1 avocado, cut in large chunks

Saute the onion in the oil. Add the broth and bring to a boil. Add the zucchini, salt, and lemon juice and cook until the squash is barely tender. Just before serving, add the avocado. Serves 4.

8
LEGUMES AND GRAINS

Cooking time for dry beans, peas, and lentils is shortened when they are soaked before cooking. However, vitamins and minerals then pass into the water so vegetables should be cooked in the water used for soaking. According to nutritionist Adele Davis, if the soybeans are frozen after they have soaked and before they are cooked, cooking time is decreased about 2 hours and they taste more like navy beans.

Sometimes I just let my beans soak in the refrigerator, thereby protecting the legumes from vitamin loss. A good rule of thumb is to use twice as much water as dry beans. In other words, if you put one cup of beans to soak, use two cups of water. I prefer to season my legumes with salt after they have been softened in cooking, although many recipes recommend putting the salt in from the start.

If the legume is not soaked before cooking, it should be dropped quickly into boiling water so that the starch grains burst and water is absorbed rapidly. This shortens the cooking time. Heat should be lowered immediately to prevent the protein from becoming tough. Just turn the reflector cooker off focus. Just a word of caution here — remove your cooking pot from the reflector stove while you are making the new adjustment. After all, it isn't quite like a countertop stove, and you don't want beans all over the ground. A simmering temperature should then be maintained for the remainder of the cooking time. With a little practice and experience you will soon learn to adjust your reflector cooker so that you won't need to check on it more than once every hour or so.

Never put soda in your cooking water if you wish to maintain your maximum vitamin B content. If salt, fat, or molasses are added at the beginning of cooking, the cooking time is prolonged. Add these ingredients *after* the legumes are tender.

Soybeans differ from other beans in that they contain about three times more protein, a small amount of sugar, and no starch. They supply essential amino acids, calcium, and B vitamins. Although relatively new to Americans, they are now available as dried green soybeans which many have found to be more delicious than other varieties and cook in a somewhat shorter time.

LENTILS

These are to be cooked on the reflector cooker in a 1-1/2 quart saucepan.

2 tbsp. oil
½ onion, chopped
1 small clove garlic
1 cup lentils
2 cups water
Salt
Pepper

Saute the onion and garlic in the hot oil, add the lentils and brown slightly. Add the water and seasonings and cook at least an hour; longer is better. Serve over rice. Serves 4.

SPLIT PEAS

You can substitute lentils for the split peas. You can also omit any of the vegetables or add different ones.

2½ cups meat stock or vegetable broth
1 cup dry split peas
1 onion, chopped
(½ cup chopped tomatoes)
(2 carrots, diced)
(2 stalks celery with leaves, chopped)
(¼ cup grated cheese)
1 bay leaf
½ tsp. thyme
Salt
Pepper
Butter or margarine

Bring the stock to a full boil. Drop the dry split peas quickly into the boiling broth. Reduce the heat and simmer 30 minutes, or until the peas are tender. (Turn the reflector off focus to simmer.) Add the onion, tomatoes, carrots, celery, seasonings, and butter or margarine. Cook until the vegetables are tender. Sprinkle with cheese before serving. Serves 4 - 6.

COOKED SOYBEANS

This recipe is for plain cooked beans. You can add seasonings and even jazz up the soybeans to taste like a delicious chili bean soup by adding tomato puree, a tablespoon of chili, and a teaspoon of cumin along with salt and pepper to taste.

1 cup dry soybeans
2 cups water or vegetable broth

Soak the beans in water in refrigerator overnight, or if convenient, soak in an ice tray 2 hours or longer. Bring 2 cups of water or vegetable broth to a boil over the reflector cooker and drop the soybeans into the water. The water will return immediately to a boil, so take the pot off the stove and turn the cooker so that it is slightly off focus. Replace the pot of beans, cover with a lid and let simmer covered for about four hours. Add water when needed. Serves 4.

ROASTED SOYBEANS

A really fun way to fix soybeans is to roast them in your solar oven. They can be seasoned so many different ways and are quite like nuts to eat. They can be used for snacks between meals or are nice as a party appetizer.

1 cup dried soybeans
2 cups water
1/4 cup olive oil
Salt or garlic salt

Soak beans in water overnight in the refrigerator. Next morning pour off the excess water and dry the beans with a paper towel. Spread the soybeans in a large flat pan and put in your solar oven at 200°. (This could be your cloudy day cooking.) Leave the beans for three hours, stirring occasionally. Then add olive oil and salt or garlic salt to taste and cook another 15 minutes. Store in an airtight container. If your roasted soybeans aren't dry enough, or if they collect moisture from the air, place them in the oven at 300° for another half hour. I like to add sunflower and/or sesame seeds to these beans. Sometimes I spice them up with a tablespoon of chili powder. Creative cooks can probably think of many other ways to garnish them. They are so delicious!

DRIED BEANS

2 cups dry navy, lima, kidney or pinto beans
1 quart water
1 - 3 tsp. salt
½ tsp. pepper
3 - 4 tbsp. vegetable oil

Soak beans in water overnight in the refrigerator. Bring to a boil over the reflector cooker and simmer for 2 to 2-1/2 hours or until tender. Add water as needed. After the beans are tender, season with salt, black pepper, and vegetable oil. Serves 4.

OVEN RICE

I use a natural rice, so it takes longer to cook than processed rice. If you're cooking on a low-sun day cook the rice longer than called for in the recipe.

2 cups water
1 cup rice
1 tsp. salt

Combine the ingredients and place uncovered in a 300° oven for one hour and 15 minutes. The rice is done when the water is cooked away and the rice looks dry.

HAPPY DAYS RICE

1 cup rice
1½ cups boiling water
2 tsp. salt
3 eggs
½ cup butter, softened
12 oz. can bean sprouts, drained
1 cup chopped green onions, bottoms and tops
⅓ cup pimentos
Dash pepper

Before assembling the above ingredients, place a pan of water, large enough to hold mold, in the oven to start heating. Boil rice in 1 cup water and 1 tsp. salt over the reflector cooker. When done, drain well. Whip the eggs in butter and add to rice. Add bean sprouts, onions, pimentos, 1 tsp. salt and pepper. Mix well and pack into a well-greased mold. I use an aluminum salad mold tube pan. Set in pan of hot water and steam for about an hour and 15 minutes at 300°. It's done when a knife inserted into the mixture comes out clean.

BULGUR

This grain is exceptionally high in nutritional value and can be prepared much the same way as rice. So whenever rice is used, for a new taste treat, try this delicious wheat grain. It can be prepared either in the solar oven or on the reflector cooker. This recipe is to be used on the reflector cooker.

1 cup bulgur
2 cups cold water
½ tsp. salt

Place water in a small cooking pot, add salt and bulgur. Cover, bring to boil, reduce heat and simmer for 15 minutes. Serves 4 - 6.

HOPPING JOHN

1 16 oz. pkg. shelled blackeyed peas
3 tbsp. vegetable oil
1 cup finely chopped onion
1 clove garlic, minced
1 cup raw bulgur
3 cups broth or water
1½ tsp. salt

In a small frying pan heat the oil and saute the onion and garlic. Set aside. Put water in a 1 qt. saucepan, place on the reflector plate, and bring to a boil. Drop the peas into the boiling water and add the salt; cook for 15 - 20 minutes. Then add the bulgur, onion, and garlic and cook slowly for another 15 minutes. Serves 6.

9
CASSEROLES

The nice thing about casseroles is that they are convenient. You can prepare several of them at one time and freeze them. This is one way that working women use the solar oven. They take a frozen casserole from the freezer and put it in the oven before leaving for work with the oven focused at the noontime direction. It defrosts, cooks, and stays warm until evening.

I like to use a casserole for our evening meal in the summertime. I start cooking the casserole at 3:00 in the afternoon when the sun is still high enough to give me a good oven temperature, cook my casserole for the required time, and then let the sun move off focus to keep the casserole warm until we eat at 5:30.

It is so easy to cook casseroles in the solar oven, as a constant temperature is not critical. Many times a casserole is much better when cooked slowly. Here is a meal you can cook later in the day, or on a day that isn't the sunniest.

BROCCOLI AND RICE CASSEROLE

1 lb. fresh broccoli, cooked and drained
2 cups cooked rice
1 10¾ oz. can cream of chicken soup
1 cup shredded cheddar cheese
1 2 oz. can water chestnuts, drained or ½ cup slivered almonds
½ cup cracker crumbs
2 tbsp. butter, melted

Add the cheese to the hot cooked rice; stir well. Add broccoli, soup, and almonds or water chestnuts. Combine the cracker crumbs with the melted butter and sprinkle over top of casserole. Bake at 300° for an hour. Serves 4 - 6.

QUICHE LORRAINE

This is a favorite recipe of our daughter Jessica. It's delicious and easy to make. Use the oil pastry recipe in the dessert section for the crust. Precook the crust for 30 minutes.

>   *¾ cup mayonnaise*
>   *2 tbsp. flour*
>   *2 eggs*
>   *8 oz. gruyere cheese, cubed*
>   *2 tbsp. Bac-O-Bits*

Blend the flour into the mayonnaise. Beat in the eggs and cheese. Pour into a 9" pie shell and sprinkle Bac-O-Bits on top. Bake at 300° - 325° for one hour. You can reheat this pie or even serve it cold. Serves 6.

Variations:

>   *½ cup celery, chopped*
>   *½ cup scallions, chopped*
>   *6 oz. package crab meat, drained*
>   *6 oz. package shrimp, drained*

Combine all or part of the above with the cheese mixture and pour into the pie shell.

CHILI RELLENOS BAKE

I call this my rainy-day special because I baked it on one of our more overcast days. Ordinarily it would have been done in an hour, but since the oven temperature never got up over 225°, I left it in for two hours. Is it ever delicious! I believe this is one of my favorite casserole main dishes. It is even good the next day served cold.

>   *2   4 oz. cans green chilis, drained and seeded*
>   *6 oz. sharp cheddar cheese, shredded (1½ cups)*
>   *1½ cups milk*
>   *4 eggs, beaten*
>   *¼ cup flour*
>   *½ tsp. salt*

Layer the chili halves in an 8" square casserole; sprinkle with cheese. Make alternate layers of chilis and cheese. Combine remaining ingredients and beat until smooth. Pour over the chilis and cheese. The casserole is done when a knife inserted comes out clean. Serves 4 - 6.

CHILI BEEF CASSEROLE

Custard casseroles don't need much attention. They seem to be made for solar cooking. You can cook them until they're firm and leave them in the oven, off focus, to keep them warm.

½ lb. ground beef
½ cup chopped onion
½ tsp. salt
¼ tsp. pepper
2 4 oz. cans green chilis, halved and seeded
1½ cups shredded cheddar cheese
¼ cup flour
½ tsp. salt
4 eggs, beaten
1½ cups milk

Brown beef and onion in skillet; drain off fat. Sprinkle meat with salt and pepper. Place half the chilis in a 10'' x 6'' baking dish, sprinkle with cheese, and top with meat mixture. Arrange remaining chilis over meat. Mix flour and salt in bowl. Combine eggs and milk. Add egg mixture to flour gradually, beating until smooth. Pour over meat and chili mixture. Cook in 300° oven for about an hour. It's done when a knife inserted comes out clean. Let cool 5 - 10 minutes; cut in squares to serve. Serves 8.

ENCHILADA CASSEROLE

This casserole is made with turkey or chicken, so you can start from scratch or use leftover turkey.

2 - 3 cups deboned chicken or turkey, cut in small pieces
1 onion, chopped
1 7 oz. can whole green chilis
1 pt. sour cream
10¾ oz. can cream of chicken soup
1 dozen corn tortillas
1 cup shredded cheddar cheese

Tear the corn tortillas into bite-size pieces and place half of them on the bottom of greased 2 quart casserole. Add a layer of turkey or chicken and a layer of chopped onions and green chilis. Make another layer starting with the tortilla pieces. Mix together the sour cream and cream of chicken soup and pour over the top. Sprinkle with cheddar cheese. Bake for an hour at 300° or better, or until bubbly. Serves 6 - 8.

LASAGNA

¼ cup olive oil
½ cup minced onion
2 garlic cloves, crushed
1 lb. ground beef
½ lb. pork sausage
1 tbsp. sweet basil
1 tbsp. salt
½ tsp. pepper
1 12 oz. can tomatoes
1 6 oz. can tomato paste
3 tbsp. parsley
1 lb. lasagna noodles
1 lb. mozarella cheese, shredded
1 lb. ricotta cheese
2½ oz. Parmesan cheese

Brown beef, pork, onion, and garlic in oil. Add seasonings, parsley, tomatoes, and tomato sauce; simmer 1/2 hour over reflector cooker. Cook lasagna as directed, drain, and rinse. Using a 2 quart casserole, alternate layers of lasagna, meat, and cheese; end with a layer of meat. Use Parmesan on top only. Bake at least one hour or until bubbly. Serves 8 - 10.

PEGGY'S EGGPLANT

Here is a nice recipe that can be used as a vegetable casserole, or you can add hamburger to it and use it as a main dish. I like it because I have a passion for eggplant, and also because it is a casserole that doesn't call for a filler, like noodles or rice.

3 eggs, hard-boiled
¾ cup garlic bread crumbs
5 tbsp. butter
1 clove garlic, minced
1 medium eggplant, peeled
2 medium bell peppers, coarsely chopped
½ cup chopped onions
1½ tsp. salt
¼ tsp. pepper
½ cup ricotta cheese
¾ cup milk

Melt 3 tbsp. butter; saute the garlic, onions, and bread crumbs in the butter. Cut the eggplant into 1'' cubes. Combine the eggplant, green pepper, and seasonings with sauteed ingredients in casserole dish. Scald the milk and add 2 tbsp. of butter; pour over the casserole mixture. Sprinkle the top with ricotta cheese. Bake at 300° for 55 minutes. Serves 4 - 6.

MANICOTTI

When preparing this dish, use the noodles in their uncooked form as it's so much easier.

Sauce

2 tbsp. vegetable oil
½ large onion, chopped
2 cloves garlic, minced
½ bell pepper, chopped
1 16 oz. can stewed tomatoes
1 15 oz. can tomato sauce
1 tbsp. basil
2 tsp. salt

Saute the onion in the vegetable oil; add garlic, pepper, tomatoes, tomato sauce, basil, and salt. Simmer until slightly thickened, about 15 - 20 minutes.

Stuffing

1 cup shredded mozzarella cheese
1 cup creamed cottage cheese
½ cup mayonnaise or 1 egg
2 tbsp. basil
1 tsp. garlic salt
12 manicotti noodles, uncooked
¼ cup Parmesan cheese

Combine all of the ingredients except the Parmesan cheese; stuff the noodles with the cheese mixture. Pour half of the sauce in the bottom of a 9'' x 13'' pan. Put the stuffed noodles on top of the sauce and cover with the remaining sauce; sprinkle Parmesan cheese over sauce. Place in a large oven bag and cook 45 minutes in a 300° - 325° oven. Remove from the bag and return to the oven for 15 minutes. Serves 6 - 8.

GNOCCHI

¾ *cup corn meal*
2 cups milk or water
1 egg
1 cup grated mozzarella cheese
1½ tsp. salt
Parmesan cheese
½ *cup vegetable oil*
2 cloves garlic
½ *cup chopped onions*
1 6 oz. can tomato paste
2½ cups stewed tomatoes
1 tsp. salt
¼ *tsp. pepper*

Put corn meal in saucepan and gradually add milk or water. Cook at low heat over reflector cooker, stirring constantly until mixture thickens and comes to a boil. Boil 3 minutes. Remove from heat, add egg and beat well. Add the mozzarella cheese, salt and 1/4 cup of the oil. While still hot, pour into an 8" square pan. Let cool; then cut into 4" squares. Arrange the squares in a 9" x 13" pan with space between for the tomato sauce. Heat the remaining 1/4 cup of oil in a saucepan, add garlic, and cook for 8 minutes. Remove the garlic from the oil and add the onions, tomato paste, stewed tomatoes, salt, and pepper. After heating for a few minutes, pour around the corn meal squares and sprinkle the top with Parmesan cheese. The yellow of the corn meal should show, so that you have islands of yellow in the red tomato sauce. Bake at 300° for one hour. Serves 6.

CANNELONI

Stuffing

1 lb. spinach
1 8 oz. pkg. lasagna noodles
2 tbsp. melted butter
1 cup small curd cottage cheese
¼ *tsp. nutmeg*
¼ *tsp. basil*
2 tbsp. Parmesan cheese
2 eggs, beaten
½ *tsp. salt*
Dash pepper

Cook the spinach and drain well; chop and cool. Cook the noodles and cut in half widthwise. Combine the remaining ingredients with the chopped spinach; put one tablespoon of the mixture in the middle of each noodle and roll up. Place seam side down in casserole.

Sauce

¼ cup butter
¼ cup flour
½ tsp. salt
¼ tsp. cayenne pepper
2 cups milk

Melt butter in a saucepan. Combine salt and pepper with flour; when the butter is bubbly add flour slowly, stirring constantly. Pour in milk; stir constantly until sauce thickens, about one minute. Pour sauce over stuffed noodles.

Topping

3 tbsp. crushed garlic croutons
3 tbsp. grated Parmesan cheese
2 tbsp. melted butter

Sprinkle topping over sauce and noodles. Bake in hottest possible oven for about one hour. Serves 6.

10
POULTRY AND FISH

Turkey

If you want to really amaze your friends, put a turkey in the oven as soon as you have any sun in the morning, attend church, then invite some friends home for dinner. When they see you take that nice, brown turkey from the oven they'll never stop exclaiming over the miracle of cooking with the sun.

If you let your oven warm up first to 350°, when you place your meat in the oven (your solar oven will take a bird 10 - 14 lbs.) the temperature will drop 50° - 75°, and fluctuate between 275° - 325°. My first 12-lb. turkey cooked in 3 hours, which is about 15 minutes per pound. This was a little faster than I sometimes like to cook a turkey, but it is a guideline for you. If you want your turkey to cook slower, simply keep the oven a little off focus. If you want the turkey to cook while you are away, you can aim the oven to the position the sun will be in when you want the oven to "come on."

There are many variables, but remember that with poultry, you always want your oven temperature above 150° as a protection against food poisoning. Any cook knows this, and there is no problem where solar cooking is concerned.

ROAST TURKEY BASTE

You can roast a turkey by simply placing it on a rack in a pan and possibly brushing with a little oil. If you'd rather, you can use an oven bag, or even a large, brown grocery bag. If you prefer your turkey basted, you might like to try something I learned years ago when I was a bride, before women started wrapping their turkeys in aluminum foil.

¼ cup flour
¼ cup margarine or butter, softened

Mix the margarine or butter with the flour and spread all over the turkey. Bake.

TURKEY AND RICE JUBILLETTE

Rarely do we have a turkey that we don't have at least some of it left over. Here is one recipe, others follow, that will keep turkey interesting for succeeding dinners.

3 cups turkey, cubed
3 tbsp. butter
3 medium carrots, thinly sliced
2½ cups turkey or chicken broth
¼ tsp. pepper
½ tsp. onion powder
¼ tsp. powdered curry
3 cups cooked white rice
½ cup grated cheddar cheese

Saute carrots in butter until tender; add turkey, broth, and seasonings. Oil a 2 qt. casserole dish and layer the rice and turkey in it. Pour any remaining broth over the top, then add cheese and bake about one hour at 300° - 325°. Serves 4 - 6.

DEE'S TURKEY TETRAZZINI

3 - 4 cups turkey cut in 1" chunks
¼ cup chicken or turkey fat or 2 tbsp. vegetable oil
2 tbsp. flour
½ tsp. cayenne pepper
6 cups turkey or chicken broth, or water
½ lb. mushrooms, sliced
1 egg yolk, slightly beaten
3 tbsp. light cream
8 oz. package medium wide noodles
2 tbsp. grated Parmesan
1 tsp. butter

Warm meat fat or oil in the top of a double boiler; stir in flour, salt, cayenne, and one cup of the broth. Cook, stirring until thickened. Stir the egg yolk and cream slowly into the sauce. Add the turkey and mushrooms; heat thoroughly. Meanwhile, cook noodles in remaining broth 10 minutes or until tender. Arrange noodles in a shallow baking dish and pour on the turkey mixture. Sprinkle the top with Parmesan cheese and bake 45 minutes in a 300° oven. It is done when bubbly. Serves 8.

TURKEY SOUP

There is no better way to achieve good nutrition than with soup. I have a good friend who says she never throws anything away. She saves vegetable peelings to be boiled for soup broth and leftover vegetables are either pulverized in the blender or used whole in the soup. And above all, never throw away the broth from the vegetables as it has a high vitamin and mineral content and makes delicious soup. Prepare in a 1-1/2 qt. saucepan.

3 cups turkey or chicken broth
1 cup turkey or chicken pieces
2 tbsp. brown rice
2 tbsp. chicken or turkey fat, or vegetable oil
1 small new potato, with the skin on
¼ tsp. sweet basil
¼ cup chopped onions
¼ tsp. curry
1 tsp. salt
Pepper
¼ cup orange juice
1 tbsp. white wine
½ orange, thinly sliced
2 tbsp. Parmesan cheese

Brown the onion in the fat or oil until transparent. Pulverize the potato and broth in a blender and add to the onions. Bring to a boil; add rice and cook until the rice is done. Add meat pieces and seasonings. Just before serving add the orange juice and wine. Float orange slices on top and sprinkle with Parmesan cheese. Serves 4 - 6.

TURKEY ALMONDINE

I cook this in my heavy pottery casserole. Start the pan warming in the oven before putting the casserole together, because the dish does hold the heat once warmed up.

> 2 cups cooked turkey, coarsely diced
> 4 tbsp. butter or margarine
> 4 tbsp. flour
> ½ cup chopped onion
> 2 cups milk
> 1½ tsp. salt
> 1 cup cooked peas
> ½ cup toasted slivered almonds
> 2 egg yolks
> ½ cup bread or corn flake crumbs
> 1 tbsp. butter
> 8 oz. package wide noodles
> 2 tbsp. Parmesan cheese

Melt the butter and saute the onion until it is transparent. Add flour and blend in the milk. Stir until the sauce is smooth and thickened. Stir in the turkey, peas, and half of the almonds. Beat the egg yolks with a fork; slowly stir 1/2 cup of sauce into the yolks until well mixed. Rapidly stir mixture back into the turkey sauce. Add to the noodles and pour into a 2 qt. casserole. Scatter the crumbs and then the almonds on top; dot with butter. Sprinkle with Parmesan cheese. Bake in a 300° - 325° oven for one hour. Serves 8.

Chicken

The same rules apply to chicken as to turkey when cooking in your solar oven. The main difference is that your chicken will often be cut up into pieces. However, when baking a chicken, follow the instructions in the turkey section for roast turkey.

Many people like to cook chicken with a "shake and bake," either their own combination of flour and spices or a commerical package. This works very well in the solar oven. Just coat the chicken with the shake and bake, place in a shallow baking dish, and let it cook in a pre-heated 350° oven. The temperature will drop a little when the meat is placed in the oven. Let it cook approximately the same amount of time as it would in an inside oven.

CHICKEN BARBECUE

3 lb. chicken, cut in pieces
1 medium onion, chopped
3 stalks celery, chopped
¼ cup salad oil
1 1 lb. can stewed tomatoes
¼ cup cider vinegar
¼ cup lemon juice
6 tbsp. brown sugar, firmly packed
2 tbsp. prepared mustard
2 tbsp. Worcestershire
1 tbsp. salt
1 tbsp. pepper

Saute onions and celery in the oil until translucent. Add tomatoes, vinegar, lemon juice, sugar, mustard, Worcestershire, salt, and pepper; simmer for 15 minutes, stirring occasionally. Dip chicken in the sauce and place in a shallow baking dish. Cook for 1-1/2 hours in a 275° - 300° oven. Serve with any remaining sauce. Serves 6.

CORNISH HENS

4 Cornish hens
2 cups cooked wild or brown rice
½ cup finely chopped bell pepper
½ cup minced celery
1 cup minced onion
1 tsp. salt
1 tsp. basil
1 egg, slightly beaten
¼ cup red wine
¼ cup melted butter

Combine the rice, bell pepper, celery, and onion with the seasonings and wine. Stuff into the cavity of each of the Cornish hens. Tie legs to tail and brush with melted butter. Place in a flat pan and bake at 300° for 1-1/2 hours. Serves 4.

SPAGHETTI CHICKEN

This is a recipe for chicken that is different and so good that our daughter Deirdre insisted that I place her endorsement on it. Some San Diego friends may recognize something familiar about this recipe, too.

4 lb. broiler-fryer, cut in pieces
3 tbsp. vegetable oil
½ cup chopped onion
1 clove garlic, minced
1 lb. can tomatoes
1 8 oz. can tomato sauce
1 6 oz. can tomato paste
2 tbsp. fresh parsley
3 tsp. basil
¼ tsp. pepper
8 oz. spaghetti, cooked and drained
Parmesan cheese

Heat the oil and cook onion and garlic until onion is transparent. Add remaining ingredients, except chicken, cheese, and noodles; mix well. Wash the chicken pieces and place in a shallow pan. Pour sauce over the chicken. Cook slowly for about 3 hours in a moderate oven. Remove the meat from the bones, place on noodles, and top with Parmesan cheese. Serves 6 - 8.

BESS' FABULOUS CHICKEN

An elegant company dinner, this recipe was given to us by a friend.

4 large whole chicken breasts
8 slices of bacon
2½ oz. chipped beef
1 10¾ oz. can cream of mushroom soup
½ pt. sour cream

Debone and skin the chicken breasts and cut in two. Wrap each serving with a slice of bacon. Cover the bottom of a flat greased baking pan with chipped beef. Arrange chicken on the beef. Mix soup and sour cream and pour over the entire surface. Bake at 275° for about 3 hours, uncovered. Serves 8.

CHICKEN TERIYAKI

This has been a favorite recipe of ours through the years. Prepare and serve Chicken Teriyaki over or beside rice.

2-2½ lb. chicken, cut in pieces
½ cup Teriyaki sauce
Grated ginger root, to taste

Marinate the chicken in the sauce and ginger root for 4 hours, turning frequently. Remove the chicken from the sauce and bake in 275º - 325º oven for 1 hour. Serves 6.

Fish

Many people have told me they aren't fond of fish. My family gave me some static on this until I learned that strong "fishy" odors or taste can be minimized with the use of wine, vinegar, ginger, onions, or garlic. Baked fish recipes lend themselves very well to our tastes and I actually get raving reviews for these recipes. Fish takes very little heat to cook and is great to bake in a solar oven.

BAKED HADDOCK OR SOLE

2 lbs. fish fillets
¼ cup butter or margarine
1½ cups bread crumbs
1 cup grated Monterey Jack cheese
¼ cup sherry
Salt
Pepper

Wash the fish, pat dry with paper towels, and place in a 8" square pan. Pour sherry over the fish and salt and pepper to taste. Saute the bread crumbs in the butter and sprinkle over the fish; sprinkle the cheese over the crumbs. Bake in a 300º oven for approximately 45 minutes. It's done when it flakes with a fork. Serves 4.

BAKED RED SNAPPER

> *3 lb. red snapper or other large fish, whole*
> *1 cup flour*
> *Salt*
> *Pepper*
> *2 tbsp. butter*
> *½ cup chopped onion*
> *2 garlic cloves, chopped*
> *8 oz. can tomato sauce*
> *1 tbsp. Worcestershire sauce*
> *1 tbsp. chili powder*

Combine flour with salt and pepper to taste. Dredge the fish inside and out with the seasoned flour and place in a large flat pan. Saute onion and garlic until onion is transparent. Add tomato sauce, Worcestershire sauce, chili powder, salt, and pepper. Pour the sauce around the fish and bake in a 300° oven for one hour. Time will vary according to shape of the fish. A meat thermometer should read 140°. Serves 6.

FISH BAKED IN COVERED CASSEROLE

> *2 lb. fish, preferably in one large chunk*
> *2 tbsp. butter, softened*
> *¼ tsp. nutmeg*
> *3 tbsp. sherry*
> *3 tbsp. butter, melted*
> *2 tbsp. capers*
> *Chopped parsley*
> *Salt*

Have fish at room temperature. Combine 2 tbsp. butter, nutmeg, and sherry; rub into fish on all surfaces. Place fish in a casserole with a closely fitting lid. Bake at 300° until tender. Do not overcook. Combine melted butter, capers, parsley, and salt. Pour over baked fish when removed from oven. Serves 4 - 6.

11
MEAT

The solar oven lends itself beautifully to cooking meat. The timing for cooking meat will be close to what it is in your inside oven. You could very easily have more heat than you want in cooking your beef, as meat cooked at low temperatures tastes better and is more nutritious. Meats cooked slowly need little watching or work. In cooking meats two temperatures must be kept in mind — the temperature inside the meat, and the external temperature. A meat thermometer is an inexpensive way to be sure about your meat. Use according to meat thermometer directions.

In cooking roast beef, leg of lamb, or pork roast, remember that salt draws the juices from the meat; it is not advisable to season your meat before or during the roasting process. You really don't need to do anything to the meat, but you can brush a little oil on the meat to help seal in the juices. Interestingly, according to nutritionist Adele Davis, the old concept of sealing in the juices by searing the roast or steak is a fallacy. Instead, essential amino acids are broken apart by the heat and their health-promoting value is decreased.

You can pre-heat the oven, if you like. Something I have found that works very well for me is to put the roast in the oven and then focus the oven ahead at the place where you want it to "come on." For example, if I were to leave for church at 9:00 in the morning and wanted a 7 lb. roast to be done when I got home from church at 12:30, I would aim the oven at the 10:30 position. If it was an overcast day and the roast wasn't quite done when I arrived home, I would just reposition the oven and cook the roast a while longer. Many times I put vegetables in with the roast, which helps to keep the temperature lower. The more bulk you have in the oven, the more it pulls the temperature down. If you're late returning home, the sun gradually moves off the oven, so the temperature is gradually dropping. I won't say you *can't* burn the meat, but your chances are better that the meat won't burn in a solar oven.

In the summertime you can cook many of your evening meals in the solar oven. If you are cooking a roast or turkey, do start by 3:00 in the afternoon, as the sun is quite low by 4:30 or 5:00 and your oven temperature will begin to decrease.

If you are going to cook steak or hamburgers, your reflector cooker is the way to go. You have an instant 500° temperature with this cooker. One day in April at 4:30 in the afternoon, I set up the reflector cooker and placed my frying pan on the grill and went inside to get three little filets. When I returned and put them in the pan, they sizzled immediately. They cook fast, too, so watch that you don't get them too well done. The grill isn't large enough to cook for a crowd, but for our family of three, three hamburger patties, or three 1'' thick filets work very well. If you want to cook hot dogs, use long forks and hold them over the grill.

SUN DOGS

> *8 beef hot dogs*
> *2 1 lb. cans barbecue beans*
> *½ cup catsup*
> *¼ cup chopped bell pepper*
> *½ cup chopped onion*
> *1 tsp. chili powder*
> *¼ cup barbecue sauce*
> *8 oz. Monterey Jack cheese, shredded*

Pour beans into baking dish. Combine catsup, bell pepper, onion, barbecue sauce, and chili powder. Slash hot dogs diagonally in several places. Place hot dogs on beans; cover with sauce. Top with shredded cheese. Bake for 45 minutes in a 275° oven. Serves 6 - 8.

SOLAR STEW

Here is a recipe given to me by one of my favorite neighbors. She said it was a favorite with them, and it proved to be just as well-received by my family.

> *2 lbs. stew meat*
> *1 package onion soup mix*
> *½ cup red wine*
> *10¾ oz. can cream of mushroom soup*
> *¼ cup lemon juice*
> *1 lb. bag frozen mixed vegetables*

Combine all of the ingredients, except frozen vegetables, in a covered casserole. Bake slowly in a 250° oven for 3 hours. Or cook it all day at a lower temperature. Add a package of frozen mixed vegetables near the end of the cooking time. Serves 4.

SWISS STEAK AND VEGETABLES

3 lbs. round steak, 1½" thick
½ cup flour
Salt
Pepper
¼ cup vegetable oil
6 whole new potatoes
6 - 10 carrots
1 onion, quartered
2 cups water or vegetable broth

Season the meat with salt and pepper, coat it with the flour, and pound well with a meat pounder or the edge of a saucer. Cut into serving pieces and brown in hot oil. Remove from the oil when brown and place in a casserole dish or shallow pan. Cover with 2 cups of hot water or leftover vegetable broth. Put new potatoes, carrots, and onion on top of the meat. Bake in the solar oven for 3-1/2 hours. Temperature can vary from 225° - 300°. Make gravy of juice left in the pan. Serves 6.

BEEF STRIPS ORIENTAL

1 lb. flank steak (partially frozen)
4 tbsp. dry sherry
4 tbsp. soy sauce
5 tbsp. vegetable oil
2 cloves garlic, crushed
1 onion, quartered
2 medium bell peppers, cut in wedges
2 tomatoes, cut in wedges
1 tbsp. cornstarch
1 cup vegetable broth

The steak is partially frozen for easy slicing. Cut the meat into paper-thin strips, almost at right angles to the grain. Combine with the marinade made of sherry, soy sauce, and 2 tbsp. vegetable oil. Set aside. Saute the garlic in 3 tbsp. hot oil; discard the garlic. Add onion, bell pepper, and tomatoes and heat until hot. Set aside. Cook the meat and marinade quickly, until meat is done. Dissolve cornstarch in vegetable broth, add to meat, and cook until thickened and bubbly. Combine with the onion, peppers, and tomatoes; serve over rice. Serves 4.

SWEET 'N SOUR MEAT LOAF

Meat Loaf
1½ lbs. ground meat
⅓ cup milk
2 eggs, beaten
½ cup minced onion
1 tsp. celery salt
¼ tsp. pepper
1 tbsp. Worcestershire sauce
1 tbsp. prepared mustard
3 slices bread, crumbled

Combine milk, eggs, and seasonings. Add bread; crumble in beef and mix well. Shape into loaf and place in pan. Cover with Sweet 'N Sour sauce.

Sauce
½ cup chili sauce
2 tbsp. brown sugar
1 tsp. prepared mustard
1 tsp. horseradish

Mix ingredients well. Cover meat loaf with sauce and bake 1-1/2 hours at about 275°. Serves 4.

MEXICAN BEEF

This is a dish common to the southwest. It is usually called Beef Burros or Burritos.

Filling
1 4-lb. chuck roast
1 4 oz. can green chilis, diced
Taco sauce to taste
1 doz. medium flour tortillas
1 cup shredded cheddar cheese

After the roast is cooked in the solar oven for 2 or 3 hours at a low temperature (225° - 300°), it should be very tender. Drain off any excess fat and break the meat apart and shred with a fork. Next mix with the green chilis and taco sauce. Put about 3 tbsp. of meat in the middle of a tortilla and fold the sides in and roll up neatly. Repeat this process with each tortilla and place in a shallow pan. Place in the solar oven and heat for 20 - 30 minutes.

Sauce

 1 1-lb. can stewed tomatoes
 ½ onion, minced
 ½ bell pepper, diced
 2 tsp. chili powder
 ½ tsp. cumin

Combine the ingredients and heat on the reflector cooker. Serve 2 burros to each person, topping with some of the sauce and sprinkled with cheese. Serves 6.

SUNNY SOUTHERN POT ROAST

 1 5 lb. pot roast
 ¼ cup flour
 1½ tsp. salt
 1 tsp. ginger
 ½ tsp. allspice
 ¼ tsp. pepper
 3 tbsp. bacon drippings
 8 oz. can tomato sauce
 ½ cup cider vinegar
 ¼ cup diced mushrooms
 2 medium onions, sliced
 2½ tbsp. sugar
 1 bay leaf

Mix flour and seasonings and coat the roast, rubbing in well. Brown well in bacon drippings. (It is easier to do this on the inside range.) Place in large pan, pour on the remaining ingredients, first blending to combine flavors. Cook slowly in solar oven for at least 3 1/2 hours. Your temperature can vary from 250° - 325°. Serves 8.

BEST EVER BARBECUE BEEF

6 lbs. chuck roast
3 large onions, chopped
2 stalks celery, chopped
2 large bell peppers, chopped
6 tbsp. barbecue sauce
1 20 oz. bottle catsup
1½ cups water
3 tbsp. vinegar
Salt
Pepper

Cut up meat in small pieces and discard bone and fat. Combine the remaining ingredients. Put in a small porcelain roaster and cover with mix. Cook about 6 hours at 250°. Fork meat apart and take out fat. Refrigerate overnight and reheat to use.

LAMB ROAST

Leg of lamb
½ cup flour
Garlic or lemon
Salt
Pepper

Remove the roast from the refrigerator at least 1/2 hour before cooking. Pre-heat solar oven to 350°. Rub the lamb with garlic or lemon and dredge with flour. Place the lamb, fat side up, in a pan on a rack in the solar oven. Bake at 300° or less. At that temperature, the leg of lamb will require about 30 - 35 minutes per pound. Season with salt and pepper. Serve with mint jelly.

PORK CHOPS AU SOLEIL

4 pork chops
½ cup apple juice
1 tbsp. brown sugar
2 tsp. or 2 cubes instant bouillon
1 tbsp. cooking oil
½ tsp. caraway seed
½ small cabbage, cut in wedges
2 apples, cored, cut in wedges
¼ cup finely chopped onion

Lightly brown chops in oil in frying pan. Put browned chops in 8"
square pan. Dissolve bouillon in hot apple juice. Combine with the remaining ingredients, and pour over pork chops. Cook in a 300° oven or less until
beautifully browned and bubbly. Serves 2 - 4.

FRUIT-STUFFED PORK LOIN

This is a really exotic company dinner.

7 lb. pork loin roast
6 oz. package prunes, pitted
6 oz. package dried apricots
1 cup dark raisins
1 cup light raisins
2 cups water
1 cup brown sugar
1 bay leaf
Salt
Pepper

Buy loin of pork; have loin cut from the bone and flat like a jelly roll.
Salt and pepper to taste. Cook the dried fruit in the water; add the brown
sugar and bay leaf to the fruit and cook until syrupy. Drain off the liquid
and save. Lay the meat out flat and spread with the fruit. Roll up like jelly
roll and tie securely with string. Roast very slowly in a 250° oven. It will
take about 35 minutes per pound. Use any extra fruit and syrup as a sauce
to serve over individual portions of the roast. Serves 6.

BAKED HAM

1 cup brown sugar
2 tsp. dry mustard
¼ cup pineapple juice
15 oz. can pineapple slices
¼ cup whole cloves

Bake the ham on a rack uncovered in a 300° oven. Allow 30 - 35 minutes per pound. It is done when the meat thermometer registers 170°. An hour before the ham is done, remove and cover with a glaze. Mix together the brown sugar, mustard, and pineapple juice; spread the mixture over the ham. Pin the pineapple slices to the ham with toothpicks and dot with whole cloves. Return the ham to the solar oven to cook for another hour.

MORE

This is a favorite recipe that our family has liked for years. We call it More simply because that's what you want after the first helping. You can make this for a crowd, or put it in a couple of family-size pans, and freeze.

½ lb. hamburger
½ lb. sausage meat
1 1-lb. can whole-kernal corn or three fresh ears of corn
2 oz. jar of pimentos
10¾ oz. can tomato soup
15 oz. can tomato sauce
6 oz. can olives, sliced in large pieces
2 large onions, chopped
2½ oz. can mushrooms or ½ lb. fresh
1 1-lb. extra-wide large noodles
2 cloves garlic, minced
1 large green pepper, chopped
1 tbsp. Worcestershire sauce
1 tbsp. chili powder
½ lb. cheddar cheese, grated
Salt

Cook the noodles on the solar hot plate according to the directions on the package. Cook meat along with the onions and drain off all the fat. Combine the rest of the ingredients together except the cheese and add to the noodles. Pour into a very large casserole or two smaller casserole dishes. hours. Serves 8 - 10.

12
DESSERTS

Many people are surprised to see that the solar oven can actually bake cakes and pies. It was a real revelation to learn that I could cook many kinds of cakes at temperatures as low at 300° — everything from a rich fudge cake to an angle food cake. Of course there are times when the oven will be hotter than 300° but it is nice to know that you don't need 350° and higher for desserts.

When baking cakes or pies you should cook them on the sunniest days, in the middle of the day if possible. I also recommend that the novice solar cook start with something simple like cookies or Apple Crisp and work up to the more difficult cakes and pies. Dark metal pans work best for me but you can use Pyrex if you prefer.

I'll admit that when I first started cooking desserts in the solar oven I had misgivings, but now it's become as easy as pie. We often plan to give such treats to friends and neighbors but most of them never leave our house. My family seems to be developing an incurable sweet tooth.

Happy solar baking. Don't let it go to waist!

PEARS CONTINENTAL

4 large pears
¼ cup toasted almonds, chopped
1 tbsp. butter, melted
2 drops almond extract
¾ cup sherry

Halve and core pears. Mix together the almonds, butter, and almond extract; put filling in the pear cavities. Put the pear halves in a baking dish, pour the sherry over them, and bake at 300° for 45 minutes. Serve hot or cold. Serves 4.

PEAR CRISP

My family likes to use fruit as a dessert. This is one of our favorite desserts and it's so easy.

6 pears
½ cup flour
½ cup brown sugar
¼ cup butter or margarine
1 cup chopped nuts
Pinch of salt

Core the pears, leaving on the skin; cut each pear into eighths. Place in a 7'' x 10-3/4'' x 1-1/2'' pan. Blend the remaining ingredients, except nuts, with your fingers and sprinkle over the pears. Top with nuts and bake 45 minutes in a 300° oven. Serve hot or cold; top with whipped cream or Kahlua. Serves 6.

APPLE CRISP

3 cups sliced apples
1¼ cups raw brown sugar
1½ tbsp. flour
Pinch salt
Pinch cinnamon
¼ tsp. baking soda
¼ tsp. baking powder
¾ cup flour
¾ cup oatmeal
½ cup margarine

Peel and slice the apples. Combine slices, 1/2 cup sugar, 1-1/2 tbsp. flour, salt, and cinnamon; place in a 2 qt. casserole. Mix remaining ingredients with your fingers until blended. Spread over apples. Bake about 1 hour in 300° oven or until the top is crusty. Serves 6.

STRAWBERRY SAND TARTS

1 cup butter
½ cup powdered sugar
2½ cups flour
2 tsp. vanilla
¾ cup finely chopped pecans
1 cup strawberry jam

Blend the butter, flour, vanilla, and pecans together; make the dough into little balls and place on sheet pan. Make a hole in each cookie with your thumb. Put strawberry jam, or any jam that has a nice, bright color, in the hole and bake for 20 - 30 minutes at 300°. After removing from the oven, dust with powdered sugar by setting them in the sugar while cookies are still warm. Makes 50 cookies.

SESAME SEED COOKIES

You can toast the sesame seeds by placing them in a frying pan on the reflector cooker. Do not add oil. Stir seeds constantly until brown.

1 cup sesame seeds, lightly toasted
1 cup flaked coconut
¾ cup margarine or butter, softened
1 cup natural brown sugar
1 egg
1 tsp. vanilla
2 cups unbleached white flour
1 tsp. baking powder
½ tsp. baking soda
½ tsp. salt

Beat together the margarine or butter, brown sugar, egg, and vanilla. Sift together the flour, baking powder, baking soda, and salt; add the sifted ingredients to the butter mixture. Stir in the sesame seeds and coconut. Drop by the teaspoonful onto ungreased cookie sheet and flatten with a fork. Bake in a 325° oven for 20 - 30 minutes. Makes 4 dozen cookies.

BETTY'S MOLASSES SUGAR COOKIES

¾ cup shortening
1 cup sugar
¼ cup molasses
1 egg
2 cups flour
½ tsp. ground cloves
½ tsp. ground ginger
1 tsp. cinnamon
½ tsp. salt
2 tsp. baking soda

Melt shortening in a 3 - 4 qt. saucepan over low heat. Remove from heat; let cool. Add sugar, egg, and molasses; beat well. Sift together flour, baking soda, cloves, ginger, cinnamon, and salt; add to first mixture. Mix well; chill. Form in 1'' balls, roll in granulated sugar, and place on greased cookie sheet 2'' apart. Flatten with a fork. Bake 15 - 20 minutes at 300° or better. Makes 4 dozen cookies.

BISQUOTTI

This is an unusual Italian cookie that is not real sweet. It is crisp, munchy, and very habit-forming.

½ cup peanut oil
½ cup sugar
2 eggs
1½ cups flour
1 tsp. baking powder
1 cup slivered almonds
1 tsp. anise extract

Blend the peanut oil, sugar, and eggs with a mixer for five minutes. Add the flour and baking powder which have been sifted together. Finally add the almonds and anise extract. The dough will be quite sticky. Spread it out very thin in a 10'' x 14'' cake pan. Bake for about 30 minutes at 300°; take from the oven and cut. Return to the oven and leave until the cookies are brown and quite dry. Makes 75 cookies.

BLOND BROWNIES

My daughters have always liked to make this recipe because you mix everything up in the saucepan in which you melt the butter.

¼ cup butter or margarine
1 cup light brown sugar
1 egg, beaten
¾ cup sifted flour
1 tsp. baking powder
½ tsp. salt
1 tsp. vanilla
½ cup chopped nuts

Melt butter or margarine. If margarine is used *do not* add salt. Add sugar and let cool. Add egg to the cooled mixture. Beat in the remaining ingredients. Spread in a well-oiled 8'' square pan. Bake for 45 minutes at 300°; cut in diamonds or squares. Makes one dozen brownies.

CORALEE'S DATE SQUARES

½ cup butter, softened
¼ cup sugar
1⅓ cups flour
2 eggs
½ tsp. baking powder
¼ tsp. salt
⅔ cup chopped dates
½ tsp. vanilla

Cream butter and sugar; stir in 1 cup flour until crumbly. Press into an oiled 8'' square pan. Bake for 35 minutes at 300° or until lightly browned. Meanwhile, beat brown sugar and eggs at medium speed until blended. Beat in the remaining 1/3 cup of flour, baking powder, and salt; add the dates and vanilla last. Spread over the baked layer and bake another half hour until golden brown. Cool. Makes one dozen squares.

COCONUT PECAN SQUARES

Dough

   ½ cup butter
   ½ cup dark brown sugar
   1 cup flour

Mix ingredients well and press into 8'' square pan, spreading batter evenly into the corners. Bake in 325° oven for 30 - 40 minutes or until brown.

Filling

   1 egg
   1 cup light brown sugar
   1 cup coarsely chopped pecans
   ½ cup shredded coconut
   2 tbsp. flour
   1 tsp. vanilla
   Pinch salt

Beat egg until frothy. Gradually add sugar and beat until thick. Add remaining ingredients and mix well; spread over baked crust. Bake 30 - 40 minutes in a 325° oven until brown. Sprinkle with confectioners' sugar when cool; cut into 1'' squares. Makes one dozen.

SUNNY LEMON CAKE

   White or yellow cake mix
   4 eggs
   ¾ cup water
   ¾ cup salad oil
   1 package lemon Jello
   1½ cups confectioners' sugar
   ¼ cup lemon juice

Mix first five ingredients together and beat four minutes with electric beater. Bake in a 9'' x 13'' pan at 300° for 1 hour. Combine the confectioners' sugar and lemon juice to make the icing. Prick cake all over with a fork and pour the mixture over hot cake; return to the oven for a few minutes to set icing. Serves 16.

CARROT CAKE

This is a cake that is good anytime, but especially good during the Christmas holiday season. It is also fun to cook in interesting shapes and sizes and use as a gift.

Cake

2 cups sugar
3 cups sifted flour
2 tsp. baking powder
1 tsp. salt
2 tsp. baking soda
2 tsp. cinnamon
¾ cup finely chopped nuts
1½ cups vegetable oil
4 eggs
2 cups finely grated carrots

Beat eggs; add oil and grated carrots. Set aside. Combine sugar, flour, baking powder, salt, baking soda, and cinnamon. Add nuts, mixing well. Add eggs, oil, and carrot mixture. Pour into greased and floured bundt pan, or two loaf pans. Bake in 325⁰ oven for 1 hour and 15 minutes. It will cook beautifully at a lower temperature, just adjust baking time.

Icing

6 tbsp. margarine
1 box No. 4 confectioners' sugar, sifted
1 8 oz. package cream cheese
2 tsp. vanilla

Melt butter and let cool. Cream sugar and cream cheese with the electic mixer. Add vanilla and butter; beat until smooth. Put cake in refrigerator after icing, as the icing is quite soft and inclined to run. Serves 15.

APPLESAUCE CAKE

The thing that makes this cake real good is using homemade applesauce. Just cook your apples; when they are tender, mash them up with a fork. Leave them a little chunky.

¼ cup shortening
½ cup sugar
½ cup hot water
1 cup applesauce
1¼ cups flour
1 tsp. baking soda
1 tsp. cinnamon
1 tsp. cloves
½ tsp. nutmeg
½ tsp. salt
1 cup raisins
1 cup nuts

Cream shortening and sugar. Add remaining ingredients and mix well. Bake in an 8" square greased pan at 325° for 45 minutes. The cake is done when it cooks away from the sides of the pan and the top springs back when you touch it. Serves 8.

SPEEDY SOLAR CHOCOLATE CAKE

This cake can be made in the pan you're going to cook it in.

1½ cups sifted flour
3 tbsp. cocoa
1 tsp. baking soda
1 cup sugar
½ tsp. salt
5 tbsp. cooking oil
1 tbsp. vinegar
1 tsp. vanilla
1 cup cold water

Put your sifted flour back in the sifter; add the cocoa, baking soda, sugar, and salt. Sift the ingredients into an oiled 9" square pan. Make three grooves, or holes, in the dry mixture. Into one, pour the oil; into the next, the vinegar; into the next, the vanilla. Pour the cold water over it all. Mix it until it's smooth and you can't see the flour. Bake at 300° for 45 minutes. Serves 6.

ZUCCHINI CAKE

Cake

        1 cup cooked zucchini
        1½ cups sugar
        ¾ cup cooking oil
        2 eggs
        1½ cups flour
        1 tsp. baking powder
        1 tsp. cinnamon
        ½ tsp. baking soda
        ¼ tsp. salt

Combine the first four ingredients and beat for two minutes. Sift the remaining ingredients together. Combine the two mixtures; pour into an oiled loaf pan. Bake at 300° for 1 hour, or until an inserted toothpick comes out clean.

Icing

        3 oz. package cream cheese
        1¼ cups powdered sugar
        2 tbsp. margarine
        1 tsp. vanilla

Cream the first three ingredients; add vanilla. Spread on cooled cake. Serves 8.

BLACK BOTTOM CUPCAKE

This is one of the yummiest cupcakes I've ever tasted. It's good whether you put sugar and nuts on the top or not. My daughter likes to use this cupcake for serving at children's parties because it doesn't need a messy frosting.

8 oz. package cream cheese
Dash salt
1 egg
1⅔ cups sugar
6 oz. chocolate chips
1½ cups flour
¼ cup cocoa
½ tsp. salt
⅓ cup oil
1 tsp. baking soda
1 cup water
1 tbsp. vinegar
1 tsp. vanilla
½ cup finely chopped nuts

Combine cream cheese, 1/3 cup sugar, chocolate chips, and dash of salt in a small bowl. Combine 1/3 cup sugar and nuts in a second small bowl. Put the rest of the ingredients in a third bowl and mix well. Line a cupcake tin with paper baking cups; fill 1/3 full with cake mixture. Add a large tbsp. of the cheese filling and sprinkle with sugar and nuts mixture. Bake for 45 minutes in a 300° oven, or until a toothpick inserted in cakes comes out clean. Makes one dozen cupcakes.

APRICOT CHEWIES

This is my favorite cookie recipe because it is so easy, tasty (company good), and nutritious too.

6 oz. dried apricots
3 cups shredded coconut
14 oz. can sweetened condensed milk

Put apricots through the meat grinder on coarse or chop well. Mix all the ingredients together and drop from a teaspoon onto a buttered cookie sheet. Bake at 300° for 25 minutes or until toasty on top. Remove at once to a cooling rack. Makes 60 cookies.

OIL PASTRY

When baking a pie that calls for an uncooked pie shell, I give it a running start in the solar oven for about 20 minutes at 300° or better.

2 cups flour
1½ tsp. salt
½ cup salad oil
5 tbsp. cold water

Sift together flour and salt. Pour salad oil and cold water into measuring cup. *Do not stir.* Add all at once to the flour mixture and stir lightly with a fork. Form into two balls; flatten dough slightly. Roll each ball between two 12" squares of waxed paper. (Dampen table slightly so paper won't slip). Peel off top sheet of waxed paper and fit dough into pie plate. Makes two 9" crusts.

GRAHAM CRACKER PIE CRUST

1⅔ cup graham cracker crumbs
¼ cup sugar
¼ cup butter or margarine, softened

Combine the ingredients. Blend well with fingers, fork, or pastry blender. Pour crumb mixture into a 9" pie pan. Put an 8" pie pan on top of crumbs and press firmly so that crumbs are molded to 9" pan. Remove 8" pan. Bake for 10 minutes; remove to wire rack to cool. Makes one 9" pie crust.

PECAN PIE

3 eggs
⅔ cup sugar
1 cup light corn syrup
¼ tsp. salt
⅓ cup melted butter
¼ tsp. vanilla
1 cup pecan halves

Beat eggs slightly; add sugar, corn syrup, salt, butter, and vanilla. Mix thoroughly. Stir in pecan halves. Pour into a 9" pastry lined pie plate. Bake in a 300° oven for 1 hour and 15 minutes, or until set and pastry nicely browned. Makes one 9" pie.

CHOCOLATE SHOO FLY PIE

This pie is so delicious and very easy to make.

9" pie crust
½ cup molasses
½ cup boiling water
2 tbsp. cocoa
½ tsp. baking soda
½ tsp. cinnamon
½ tsp. cloves
½ cup flour
½ cup sugar
¼ cup butter, softened

Bake the pie crust in the oven for 30 minutes. Combine the molasses, water, cocoa, baking soda, cinnamon, and cloves; let stand while preparing topping. Combine flour, sugar, and butter. Pour the molasses mixture into pie shell, top with crumb mixture, and bake 40 minutes in a 300° - 325° oven. Makes one 9" pie.

CHEESE PIE

Years ago a friend shared this recipe with me, and it has been an all-time favorite with our family and anyone we've shared it with. Use a graham cracker crust.

Filling
12 oz. cream cheese
¾ cup sugar
2 eggs, beaten
1 tsp. vanilla
2 tsp. lemon juice

Allow the cream cheese to soften and beat in the other ingredients. Pour into a graham cracker pie shell and bake at 300° for 25 minutes. Cool for five minutes.

Topping
1 cup sour cream
1 tsp. vanilla
1 tsp. lemon juice
3½ tbsp. sugar

Combine ingredients and spread over the top of the cooled cream cheese pie. Bake for 15 minutes at 300°. Refrigerate. Leave the pie in the refrigerator for several hours before cutting. Serves 6.

APPLE SCOTCH PIE

This is delicious made in either a graham cracker pie shell or an oil pastry shell. If you use the oil pastry, cook it in the solar oven at 300° for 15 - 20 minutes before filling the apples. This is good with cherries, too. It also can be used without the pie crust and topped with whipped cream.

Filling
    6 medium apples or 2 1 lb. 4 oz. cans apple pie filling
    ⅔ cup brown sugar, firmly packed
    2 tbsp. flour
    2 tbsp. lemon juice
    Pinch salt
    1 9" pie shell

Peel and slice the applies. Combine in a large bowl with the other ingredients. Mix well and pour into the 9" pie shell.

Topping
    ⅔ cup flour
    ½ cup quick-cooking rolled oats
    ½ cup chopped nuts
    ¼ cup sugar
    ½ tsp. salt
    1 tsp. cinnamon
    4 oz. package butterscotch pudding (do not use the instant pudding)
    ½ cup butter, melted

Combine the ingredients in a large bowl and mix with fingers until crumbly. Sprinkle over the apples and bake in a 300° oven for one hour. Makes one 9" pie.

SOLAR EQUIPMENT AND SUPPLIES

A-Z Solar Products
P.O. Box 22688
Robbinsdale Branch
Minneapolis, Minnesota 55422
(612) 537-3616

> *Cookers*
> *Cigarette Lighters*
> *Solar Cells*
> *Reflective Material*
> *Watches*
> *Electronic Project Kits*
> *Books*
> *Sundials*
> *Solar Slide Sets*

Edmund Scientific Co.
Barrington, New Jersey 08007
(609) 547-3488

> *Cookers*
> *Cigarette Lighters*
> *Solar Cells*
> *Aluminized Mylar Sheets*
> *Sundials*
> *Books*
> *House Plans*

Kerr Enterprises, Inc.
309 East 14th Street
Tempe, Arizona 85291

> *Plans for "Solar Box Cooker"*

Sedona Solar Shop
Box 1737
Camp Verde, Arizona 86322
(602) 567-9551

> *Solar Chef Cookers*

Solar Cookers
Dan Halacy
5804 West Vista Avenue
Glendale, Arizona 85301

> *Solar Oven Kits*
> *Solar Hot Plate Kits*

Solar Pro's Inc.
2224 West Desert Cove, Suite 201
Phoenix, Arizona 85029
(602) 993-1598

    Cookers

Solar Usage Now, Inc.
Box 306
Bascom, Ohio 44809
(419) 937-2226

    Cookers
    Solar Cells
    Reflective Material
    Watches
    Books
    Sundials

Sundials & More
New Ipswich, New Hampshire 03071
(603) 878-1000

    Solar Cells
    Sundials

Sunway
611 Evergreen Street
Burbank, California 91505
(213) 846-0592

    Cookers

SUGGESTED READING

Daniels, Farrington. *Direct Use of the Sun's Power*. Ballantine Books, 1964.

Hackleman, Michael. *The Homebuilt, Wind-Generated Electricity Handbook*. Peace Press, 1975.

Hackleman, Michael. *Wind and Windspinners*. Peace Press, 1974.

Halacy, Dan. *Solar Science Projects*. Scholastic Publications, 1966.

Waugh, Albert E. *Sun Dials: Their Theory and Construction*. Dover Publications, 1973.